Far from the PEACEFUL SHORE

BY RAY LAND

Authentic and inspiring stories of a bygone era

BOOKSURGE PUBLISHING ◆ CHARLESTON, SC

Far from the Peaceful Shore:
Authentic and inspiring stories of a bygone era

Author: Ray Land, Carlisle, PA

Editor and Agent: Esther Cool,
Cottonwood, AZ

Cover and book design: Jane Perini
Layout and production: Atara Heiss
Thunder Mountain Design & Communications, Sedona, AZ

Illustrations:
Ray Land, Carlisle, PA
Don Rinehart, Don Rinehart Studios, Mechanicsburg, PA

BookSurge Publishing:
7290 B Investment Drive, Charleston, SC 29418
To order additional copies visit www.booksurge.com,
www.amazon.com or call, toll free 866-308-6235.

ISBN 978-1-4276-2803-9

CONTENTS

Early Days ❖ 1

School Days ❖ 31

ILLUSTRATIONS BY RAY LAND

ILLUSTRATIONS BY DON RINEHART

PICTURES ON SECTION DIVIDERS

Early Days:
Raymond Land – Age seven

School Days:
Altamaha School Building

Farm Work:
Picking Cotton – Jonathan, Ruth and Mary

Fun Times:
Timmy, Ray, Cindi, Jon and Steve

Sad Times:
A Sharecropper's House

Trips:
Taylor's Gully

More Stories:
Ray's former home – Jon, Cindi. Ruth
Other children belong to Lucious and Mary Thomas

Other Memories:
Mama holding Floyd, Kenneth, Grandma
Cecil is standing

DEDICATION

*To my dear wife Ruth, and our
three children Cindi, Jon and Steve as
a legacy of my life "When I was a boy".*

*To my sweet sister Faye Blair and older
brother Floyd with whom I have shared so
many wonderful experiences.*

*And to other kinfolk and friends who may
be interested in the history and harsh demands
of life during the Great Depression.
- God bless you all.
- Ray Land*

BIOGRAPHY

Ray Land was born in Hazlehurst, Ga. in 1925. He was the fifteenth child of Stephen John Land and the fifth child of Allie Myrtle Land. They lived on a farm in Appling County, Ga. for nine and a half years. Ray married Ruth Dorman in June of 1946 and the Lord blessed them with three children, Cindi, Jon and Steve. Having celebrated their 60th wedding anniversary in June of 2006, they are now enjoying their 10 grandchildren and 4 great grand children.

To include a note of interest: Ray's grandfather, an avid "Unionist", served in both the Rebel and the Union Armies during the Civil War. His great, great grandfather was with George Washington at Valley Forge, Pa. Ray is still a "history buff", and loves to visit the Civil War battlefields when he has the opportunity.

Ray and Ruth Land
Gettysburg, PA

INTRODUCTION

Born in 1925, Ray Land was a boy between five and twelve years of age during the days of the Great Depression in the early 1930's. He learned to work at a very early age—in fact WORK was a way of life for him and his family. This did not stop him and his brothers from indulging in numerous cunning schemes to outwit their parents (or so they thought) in pursuit of adventure and excitement. With no money for toys, they connived ways to have lots of fun. Many of their inventions were most unusual and clever, but some of their ideas and experiments landed them in deep trouble and the consequences were severe. They must have reasoned "Oh well, it was fun while it lasted"!

Ray married Ruth Dorman in 1946. After their three children came along, he spent many hours with his family sharing various experiences and adventures of his childhood. As the children grew up, married and had families of their own, Grandpa's opportunities started all over again. There are now 10 grandchildren and 4 great grandchildren. As his fascinating accounts were told to more and more family and friends, he responded to his wife Ruth, daughter Cindi and sister Faye's suggestion to write the stories in a book. Considered legally blind and over eighty years of age, this would be no small task. This book is truly a labor of love. It bears meaning for all classes of people, young or old, rich or poor. Relax, read and enjoy.

Ray and Ruth and I were close Christian friends when I

lived in Pennsylvania. Since my move to Arizona in 1988 our friendship has continued strong. When I received a copy of the first edition of *Far From the Peaceful Shore*, which was prepared primarily for family and friends, I could hardly wait to read it. When I did, I was impressed with the resourcefulness and humor of those people as they overcame their difficulties—it is really quite entertaining. My first thought was, "this book should be published." Many agreed. The accounts are authentic. It is a colorful portrayal of the character of people during the dark days of the Depression, as they pursued life with courage, stamina and enduring hope. This is truly a must for today's readers.

Go with us now as we look at the life and experiences of this young boy and his family in this Second Edition of *Far From the Peaceful Shore*.

I wish to give a special "thank you" to Ray's sister Faye Blair who so kindly offered to sponsor the production of *Far From the Peaceful Shore*. Without her generous help publication of this book would not have been possible. These recollections from the past by Ray Land will be treasured as a family legacy and bring enjoyment to all who are privileged to read them. May you be blessed and enriched as you reflect on the true life experiences of this young boy and his family.

A Friend,
Esther Cool

PREFACE

The stories set forth in *Far From the Peaceful Shore* are all true. No liberties were taken to enhance a particular tale. Colorful words and expressions, common to the area, are used to give the reader a feeling for the day in which these events unfolded.

After many years of sharing these stories and historic accounts with family and friends, my wife Ruth, daughter Cindi and sister Faye suggested that the narratives of my early childhood should be written down. As the project got underway my desire was to leave a legacy, not only for my kinfolk, but also for the many others who have an interest in "life" as it was in the Deep South during the Great Depression of the early thirties. By common demand these accounts have reached parameters far beyond my original expectations.

The experiences, adventures and hardships you will read about in this book took place when I was but a lad of five through twelve years of age. They were difficult days, and survival meant lots of hard work. If my brothers and I wanted toys, we made them. Our "inventions" were very unique, to say the least. As with any normal boys, our minds were always busy finding ways to have fun, by fair means or foul. And we did have fun—great fun, but not without "consequences".

At that time I did not yet know the Lord Jesus Christ as my Savior, but His watchful eye and wonderful love were set upon me long, long ago. It was He who carried me through all the dangers and difficulties of my young life. I was a boy *Far From the Peaceful Shore*.

My prayer is that all who read these accounts will be blessed, not only by the stories, but also the verses of Scripture my book contains.

In addition, a debt of gratitude is owed to Esther Cool. Had this talented lady not persevered, *Far From the Peaceful Shore* most likely would never have been published. The arduous task before her was made more difficult by the author's many changes.

Patience is not without its reward. Thank you, Esther.

Ray Land

Early Days

~ Sinking to Rise No More ~

Seated on the back of one of our mules, I was ever so slowly making my way to our neighbor's house, some two miles away, where I was to pick up three books for my mother to read. The route we were taking could scarcely be called a road, not even a path. Tar wagons would occasionally travel in this area but not often enough to wear down the tree sprouts, bushes and weeds that grew up. I was not quite sure of my direction but my companion, with her amazing instinct and having traveled this way before, allowed me to relax and give her the reins.

A breeze rustled the tops of the majestic, tall, yellow pine trees that grew in abundance. A pungent smell of pine tar and pine needles filled the air. Many kinds of birds sang merrily in the thickets and trees that surrounded us. In the distance the familiar voice of a mysterious rain crow rang out, an omen of impending rain or a storm, so I was told. Years later I learned that this legendary prophetic bird was nothing more than a woodpecker warning other woodpeckers to stay out of it's territory.

All seemed so serene and pleasant as we traveled along. Surely God had made it this way and it was wonderful. I was excited and having fun. Since I was riding high up on the mules' back instead of walking, there was no need to fear those slithering creatures that infested the woods and were often found in the thick grass under our feet.

After we arrived safely at our neighbor's farm, we enjoyed

3

a short but pleasant visit. When it was time to go, the family came out into the yard to bid me farewell. My mule was led over to a large pasture gate, which I quickly climbed and jumped onto the mule's back. The books were handed up to me and we set off for home.

My heart pounded with excitement as I thought of the pictures and stories that would be found in the books. I could hardly wait to have Mama read to me. This was a super day and could only get better. My optimism was at an all time high. We had not traveled far when suddenly a brilliant idea struck me—*we'll take a shortcut and go by the way of the old swimming hole—that way we'll be home in no time!* My older brothers and their friends had widened a rather deep stream, which resulted in a sizable pool. This presented a problem to my plan—we would have to jump the narrow end of the pool! Oh, but she could do it, *"a piece of cake"*! That was it then, *"swimming hole, here we come!"* We soon reached the path that wound its way down to the pool. Without hesitation we turned onto it and began our descent. Riding here was not easy. Trees, overhanging branches and bushes made our going difficult. Nearing the creek, I urged my mule to go at a faster pace. We would need the speed to make the big jump, or so I supposed. Suddenly, we burst out into the clearing. The pool loomed straight ahead. As we reached the edge my faithful companion, (up to now), plopped both front feet down and came to a complete stop! I was propelled like a cannon ball, out over the mule's head and into the black, murky, deep water of the old swimming hole. It is impossible to describe the utter fear and terror that came over me. In an instant I knew my situation was hopeless. I could not swim. My arms flailed madly even before I hit the water. That didn't help me—I sank immediately. Swallowing and choking on large amounts of the dark liquid I struggled to the surface, gasping for breath. Fear of

death and the fires of hell raced through my mind. Would I ever see my precious mother again? There was no one around to see my plight or hear my cries. Once more I went under. Unable to breath and getting weaker, I again managed to come to the surface. My brothers had told me that if a person went down for a third time he would not come back up. It would be curtains! Slowly my body started downward, I was "Sinking To Rise No More"! Submerged in the water, with my face turned upward, for some reason I opened my eyes. As I did, I saw the sun shining right down to where I was. *Then I saw them*! The suns rays illuminated some large roots that were coming from a tree standing at the waters edge. I reached out and grabbed one and was able to pull myself upward. Soon my head popped out of the water and I was able to make it out and onto the bank. For some time I lay there exhausted, gagging, regurgitating water. Needless to say I was most grateful to be alive!

After sufficiently recovering from the ordeal, the books became my focus. There they were lazily floating around—now about twice their normal size. Finding a long pole I began to fish them over to the shore. As I pulled them up out of the water I was ever so careful not to fall back in. Now where was my transportation? I spotted her a few yards away, munching on a patch of green grass, totally unconcerned with the events that had recently transpired. Had I drowned, it would have mattered not to this dumb beast. Putting the bridle reins over her head I led her over to a rather tall stump. Holding the books as tightly as I could, I proceeded with much difficulty to get on her back. This finally accomplished, we once more set off for home.

What would my dear mother say? The books were ruined. How would she respond when I told her my account of things? Just what kind of reception would I receive? Would my miraculous escape from a watery grave evoke strong emotions in her? Would she praise God for his merciful kindness and bathe my head with her tears as she clasped me to her bosom? Or would I receive a good whipping? As I rode along such thoughts flooded my mind. Thankfully we did arrive home, and I received both the love and the rebuke that were in order.

The title for this story, "Sinking to Rise No More, is from a hymn by James Rowe called "Love Lifted Me". Even though I remembered that terrifying experience some 72 years ago, I rarely spoke of it until I became a Christian. Now that I am saved I love to relate it.

Dear friend, I was just a little boy and in a desperate situation—unable to swim, unable to breathe, and no one around to hear my voice, even if I had been able to cry out. Being only seconds away from eternity, God in His infinite mercy had compassion and spared me. It was not "by chance" that the suns' rays revealed those tree roots which enabled me to escape a watery grave. Just so did my Savior, the Lord Jesus Christ protect and deliver me from the many dangers and fears of my childhood, even though I was not aware of it at the time. (Many of these experiences are recorded in this book.) ,

"I was sinking deep in sin
Far from the peaceful shore
Very deeply stained within
Sinking to rise no more
But the Master of the sea
Heard my despairing cry
From the waters lifted me
Now safe am I"
- BY JAMES ROWE

~ *The Big Belgian* ~

It was near evening time and things were relatively quiet. Off in the distance, the rumbling noise of an approaching vehicle could be heard. Our curiosity aroused, my three brothers and I rushed to the front of the house to see who or what

7

was coming. A short time later, a big truck pulled into the yard. It was Daddy returning from town. And guess what else we saw? There on the back of the truck was the most beautiful, the most magnificent horse we had ever beheld! We were accustomed to seeing mules, but never had we owned a horse. For a time we all just walked around admiring this fantastic animal, a Belgian draft horse.

After removing the big "B" from the truck, even though it was beginning to get dark, Daddy allowed us, one by one, to sit on the horse's large back. You could sit cross-legged without fear of falling off. *It was terrific*!

These horses are among the worlds heaviest; and can weigh up to 1700 pounds. They were bred to pull heavy loads. The first Belgians were a shiny black, but by crossbreeding, a lighter color was obtained. Ours was a light tan with a long white mane and white chest, and white around the hock area.

We soon learned that our father did not purchase the big "B" just to be paraded around. It was to work—to do *hard work*! Fitted with bridle, collar, harness, and reins, he was hitched to a large plow. Unlike the mules, he attacked his task with gusto! Pulling the plow at a fast pace, it was all that my older brother Kenneth could do to keep up. The horse was so strong he did not seem to tire. My father, observing the horse's endurance must have thought this new acquisition would prove to be very profitable.

All seemed to be going well. Suddenly, something from without, or something from within, spooked the big "B" and he began to run madly across the field, dragging the plow and my brother along with him. Kenneth was helpless to restrain this powerful animal. Reaching a barbed wire fence, the horse plowed, literally, right into it. The barbs tore at his flesh, making deep gashes on the broad chest and upper part of his front legs. With a wild crazed look in his eyes and frothing at the mouth he became more and more entangled in the fence wire. Finally he began to settle down and Daddy and my brothers managed to free the horse. It was now evident that something was very wrong with this poor creature and he would be of no further use to us as a work animal. All I remember is that not long after this experience, the Belgian, was put back onto the old truck and driven away. I had looked forward to spending a lot of time riding on his broad back. My older brothers, (especially Kenneth) likely thought differently. Keeping up with big "B" would require super effort and be very tiring, for sure. The mule's slow pace would be more to the boys liking.

Big "B" had been with us for only a few days, but in that short time, he had completely won our hearts. As we looked longingly down the road at the disappearing truck, it was a sad day!

~ The Old Rattler ~

The day was beautiful and sunny but not exceptionally hot—just warm enough to cause the Land family to seek shelter on their cool rambling porch. The swing looked very inviting and so did the rockers. As we relaxed, our peace and tranquility were suddenly shattered by an ear-piercing shout! "Look", someone was saying, "down the road!"

We were sufficiently aroused to look in the direction of a pointing finger. Although he was some 50 or more yards away, there was no mistaking this fellow! The biggest, the longest rattler our eyes had ever beheld—it was probably five feet or more in length. Everyone began running toward the deadly snake but making sure we didn't get too close lest he bite us. It was clear in our minds where he was headed.

Across the field was a large swamp. The crops had recently been harvested, so the fields were bare and the sandy soil would be hot. So, why did he not wait until the cool of the evening? Snakes are cold-blooded creatures and must regulate their own body temperatures. They do this by finding suitable locations. The field soil would cause the rattler considerable pain or discomfort. It was all very puzzling, especially since the woodsy area he had come from was probably ten to fifteen degrees cooler.

My father sent my older brother Kenneth to the house to fetch the shotgun. Quick and drastic action had to be taken. The rattler must not reach the swampy area that we crossed frequently. One unsuspecting encounter with this monster snake would be one too many.

The commotion we were making brought our neighbor and sharecropper to the scene, along with his entire family. Our two dogs, Mutt and Jeff, were also present, barking loudly. When the dogs came too close, the snake would coil and begin rattling furiously, flicking his tongue. Kenneth had not yet returned with the gun and the object of our attention was getting closer and closer to his destination. If he made it to the swamp, we would never find him –(not that I would ever look)!

Still no Kenneth and time was running out. It is here that Divine Providence becomes evident. At one time, a little patch of small trees and bushes jutted out from the swamp. People walking, riding or even with a plow would cross this narrow stretch. So a cleared space of about ten or twelve feet existed between a small copse of trees and the swamp itself. Seeing this we began yelling, throwing rocks and sticks at the snake hoping to make him enter the copse instead of the swamp. Our efforts were rewarded— the rattler did turn into it. So far, so good. I might add at this juncture, had this venomous reptile gone into the swamp, nothing could have made me venture anywhere near that place.

Finally Kenneth came running up with the gun, the gun we

hoped would be old rattler's terminator. Daddy kept circling the area in order to get a shot off but couldn't see the snake. We could all hear him rattle but...where was he? One of my brothers was dispatched to the house for a long Bamboo fishing pole. Upon his return, a neighbor took the pole and began pushing the weeds and bushes down. Suddenly Daddy spotted our adversary. BOOM! It was over.

We all gave a deep sigh of relief. It would be some time before our hearts returned to normal. One of my brothers found a long pole with which he picked the huge snake up and carried it across the field and road from which it had come. He draped the snake over a low hanging branch on a nearby persimmon tree. For a period of time, you could see its body hanging there. Eventually vultures or scavenger animals devoured the flesh, and the bones fell to the ground. I was told if you should step on one of these bones you would surely die. Needless to say I never did. This particular area was definitely off limits for me.

~ The Woman from Blarney ~

The first ten years of my life were spent on my father's farm in South Georgia. The people of that area were as a general rule hard working, honest and God fearing. These rural folk were bound together by religious ties, race, common problems, quaint ways and sayings. I count it an honor and a privilege to have been exposed to their unique culture and their strength.

My childhood was so very different from what children experience today. For example, our locale had no paved roads, no electric lights, no running water, no inside plumbing and if, while attending a one-room school, nature should call, we boys headed for the nearby woods.

Not far from our farm was a district known as Blarney,

which was populated to a large extent by black folk, or African Americans. Some of them had been former slaves. There lived in Blarney a mysterious woman. Numerous stories were circulated among the white community concerning this person. She was said to have great foretelling powers and to engage in strange rituals. When an occasion arose requiring me to pass her house, I ran as fast as my spindly legs would carry me. To say I was scared was an understatement—surely some dreadful thing would happen should she catch me. Now I am hard pressed to explain why I had such trepidation when it came to this particular woman. She had never spoken to me, nor I to her.

Then came the momentous day when the enigmatical lady from Blarney paid a visit to our home. How well I remember that eventful day. It was July 27, 1931 to be precise—some seventy six years ago. Mama had come in from the fields and gone into her bedroom. My three brothers and I were instructed to go out and sit under a pear tree and to stay there until told otherwise. Some time elapsed when in the distance

we saw a solitary figure coming down the lane. It was a black woman with a bandanna wrapped around her head, wearing a long full flowing dress. She carried a large black satchel in her hand. To our great surprise, she entered our house. I had no clue as to what was going on and no plans to find out. I was in shock!

After a considerable amount of time the woman from Blarney came out and made her way down the road in the direction from which she had come. A few minutes later Daddy appeared on the porch and called for us. We came into the house and were ushered into Mama's room. Such a sight we beheld! There cuddled in my mother's arms was a tiny pink babe, our baby sister Faye. My brothers maintained that the woman had brought this little one in a satchel from Blarney, and I was inclined to believe them. Why should I think otherwise? Lula Bell, the woman from Blarney, could work wonders, and she had.

~ A Ride to Blarney ~

When it came time to chop or pick our cotton and to cure the tobacco, we desperately needed help on our farm. One family could never accomplish such an enormous task by themselves; field workers would be required. As a little boy, it never occurred to me how dependent we were on these laborers. To obtain this necessary help, a trip to Blarney would have to be made.

My brother Floyd and I arose very early. We hastily ate a bowl of oatmeal, and if Mama's delicious biscuits were ready, we most likely made a hole in a warm one and filled it with syrup. There were few South Georgia families that did not enjoy this treat. Dashing off to the barn, the mule would be led out of the stable, harnessed, and hitched to the wagon. This done, we set off for Blarney.

How thrilling it was to be making a trip like this. The little details and happenings stand out ever so vividly in my mind—the cool refreshing early morning air, the creaking of our old wagon, the steady plodding sound as the mules' hooves struck the ground, and the first rays of the sun as they filtered through the tops of the tall pines. Oh, how I loved it all.

I sat beside my brother Floyd, who seemed so big, so mature, like a grown man, all ten or eleven years of him. It was exciting! A feeling of importance came over me. Floyd must have felt the same. We were doing something of real significance, much like our Daddy would do.

All the roads in our area were dirt. The one we were traversing was such and remains so until this present day. Coming to the mail route and what is now called Piney Bluff Road, our destination lay straight ahead, only a couple of minutes away. There we would find a clearing and a cluster of small houses. The exact number, I do not recall, perhaps five or six, maybe more. They were arranged in a kind of "U" shape with the front of the buildings facing inward. The ground surrounding these dwellings was completely barren of grass, exposing dazzling white sand.

We crossed Piney Bluff on to what could scarcely be called a path, and within a minute or so came to a stop at the opening to the little community. A fair amount of activity could be observed, a good part of which was yapping dogs. Children ran here and there, pretending not to notice us (but were very aware of our presence). Some adults were in the process of starting fires under those magnificent big pots that stood in the middle of the courtyard. These pots were used for a variety of things—heating water, cooking large amounts of food, etc.

Without the large vessels, life would be even more difficult than it presently was.

Slowly the workers began to enter the wagon. We soon finished our expressed purpose and were ready to return to the farm. As we patiently waited for the last laborer to arrive, a few words must be said about the inhabitants of this place.

The dear folk of the little community were extremely poor. They may not have regarded themselves as so, but I assure you they had little of this world's goods. Life was a struggle— a desperate one. Opportunity didn't just pass them by; there was no opportunity!

The year was 1932, a period in the Great Depression. Most white farmers were much better off than their black neighbors, materially speaking, but because of the country's economic condition, they were having a hard time of it themselves. With cotton at five cents per pound, the field hands wages were a mere pittance. I must tell you, in spite of these trying circumstances, I never heard the people of Blarney complaining.

I now consider it a distinct privilege and an honor to have been invited to dine with a poor black family. The meal consisted of a glass of water, a small amount of turnip greens, and a piece of cornpone made of corn meal, lard and water. The head of the house would bow his head, fold his black gnarled hands and say something like this, "Oh, Lord, we thank thee for this bountiful provision. Bless it to our bodies use. Amen." How absolutely wonderful! Their gratitude and their faith was amazing.

My mother and father had more than a passing interest in these people. I can remember going to the community to visit a dear soul who was afflicted with lockjaw (tetanus) and lay dying. Mama was never insensitive to the needs of her black

friends. Church was also an important factor in the lives of
these Blarney people. Many of those who attended are listed in
Ruth T Barron's book entitled "Footprints of Appling County".
The Civil War had freed the Blarney blacks and others from
slavery but provided them with little or nothing else. A number
of former bondsmen could be found here in their midst.

This little company of people had learned a wonderful
lesson—one we all need to learn. "What is that, you say?"
Simply this: contentment my friend, contentment! How very
rich were these black brethren in the Lord's sight. The Bible says,
"Godliness with contentment is great gain" (I Timothy 6:6).

Little children were often barefooted, clothed in flour-sacks, gunnysacks or other ragged and well-worn apparel. Many of them were hungry. Some were sick and unable to see a doctor because of finances. Such was the lot of most of these folks, not just the little ones.

The wagon filled with workers and we started back to the farm. Everyone was exceptionally quiet. Most had not fully awakened from their sleep. They would be reacting in a totally different manner once their workday was over.

When we arrived at the farm, the hired hands disembarked and were directed to the cotton field. Each worker was given a very long sack with a strap attached. He or she would put the strap over their shoulder, and selecting a row, they started picking. Had we arrived before the sun dried the cotton out, work would have been delayed. Dew on the cotton makes it heavier and since the picker is paid by the pounds of cotton he picks, a delay might be in order. As sacks were filled, they were taken to a nearby site where my brother Kenneth weighed the contents and dumped them into the wagon. He then recorded the pickers name and the cotton's weight.

Occasionally the picker would place a large rock in his sack to increase the weight, thereby receiving more pay for his supposed sack full of cotton. I must say Kenneth was quite sharp to discover the cheaters tactic! The culprit was promptly dispatched home without being paid.

The hands would toil all day in a boiling sun. Water was brought out in buckets along with a gourd dipper. The pickers would pause briefly at the end of a row to quench their thirst. Around noon a loud banging on a plowshare would signal them to stop for dinner. It was sad to see of what their meal consisted. A biscuit saturated with syrup, (from sugar cane), fried grits and little else. It has always amazed me how these people could survive on so little. Surely God enabled them to do so. After a short break, they resumed their picking.

Around five or six, their workday would come to an end. Since we never ever drove them home, they would start off down the road singing, joking, and laughing. The young men were forever teasing and chasing the young girls. They seemed to have no end of energy.

Most if not all of those employed by my father have now passed away. Many of these dear folk are in a land where they will never grow old. They will never again have to toil under a scorching sun. They will never hunger or thirst. Someday I will join that heavenly company from Blarney and pay the debt I owe them by saying "Thank you".

"For the Lamb...shall feed them and shall lead them unto living fountains of waters: and God shall wipe away all tears from their eyes.
– REVELATION 7:17

～ *The Porker* ～

As the weather grew colder, Daddy sensed that it was time to act. He selected a choice young pig from our hog populace. The animal was then placed in a newly constructed elevated pen. Fed a special diet, Porky, as we may have called him, grew larger and larger day by day. He was living "high on the hog", one might say. What this piggy didn't know was what his owner and benefactor had in store for him. What the owner was not aware of was that things would not turn out as planned.

The days and nights became quite cold. This would be of

little concern to Porky since he had developed a thick coat of fat and was rapidly turning into a hog. Then one bright and chilly morning, Daddy announced that his plans for Porky would be carried out that very day. After breakfast, he strolled out to view his prized porker for the last time. Looking into the pen he was aghast to find it empty. Porky had vanished!

After a moment or two, Daddy regained his composure and began looking around. There were blood droplets both inside and outside of the pen. Furthermore, it was obvious that a heavy object had been dragged out into the field behind our house. The picture was clear now; someone had killed the hog, probably with one blow from an axe. This would prevent Porky from squealing and thus awakening our family.

Returning to the house, Daddy proceeded to arm himself

with his trusty double-barreled 12-gauge shotgun, his 32-caliber colt revolver, and a large hunting knife. Thinking himself to be sufficiently outfitted, he set out to find the culprits. Considering the hog's weight, at least two must have been involved. You would not have to be a bloodhound or a Sherlock Holmes to follow the trail. Weeds were flattened down and deep depressions showed in the ground as Porky was pulled along.

Passing from our farm on to that of Offie Jones, Daddy steadily continued his tracking. Coming to Piney Bluff Road, the hog takers crossed over and made their way down a road that could lead to only one place, the little community of farm workers in Blarney.

When Daddy arrived at the entrance to the community courtyard, he beheld a joyful scene. Men, women and children were feverishly scampering about. Dogs seemed equally excited, barking continuously. Fires burned under the huge black pots. Boiling water was being drawn from them and carried over to a wooden barrel that was partly submerged in the ground at an angle. The scalding water was poured over a large object visible in the barrel. The object, as you no doubt have guessed, was a hog!

Daddy stood staring at the gleeful event before his eyes. What would be his next course of action? One thing is certain; a flood of thoughts raced through his mind. After some time and without speaking, he slowly turned and began making his way back home.

There seems to be little need to further comment on this story, except to say, some kind of poetic justice of a divine nature had occurred and Daddy never did find his hog.

~ The Caterpillar Umbrella and Cap ~

A group of men were blazing a firebreak through the woods and swamps near our farm. Cutting down the trees and underbrush would help control forest fires, should they occur.

At the end of the laborers' workweek, one of the crew drove his big yellow Caterpillar up near our barn and parked it. He asked my father if he could leave it there until Monday. Daddy said it would be fine with him.

Saturday came and we boys went out to give the big Cat a good going over. One item that did not escape our eye was a colorful umbrella, neatly folded and secured to the side of the tractor. We took turns sitting in the driver's seat making loud noises, pretending to operate the giant machine. It wasn't long until our focus was back on the umbrella. Removing it from its resting place, it was unfolded. Wow! The thing was huge! Maybe seven feet wide and it looked very much like a parachute. Almost instantly we headed for the barn, carrying the umbrella.

We climbed up into the hayloft and opened the door. It must have been thirty feet to the ground below. Many times sheets had been used to make a parachute and we all had jumped out hoping for a soft landing. The results were always pretty much the same, sprained ankles, sore hands or knees.

This jump was going to be different. It would simply be super. Kenneth, being the oldest, bailed out first. We stood with baited breath as he leaped out into the wild blue yonder. Kenneth had hardly left the door opening when the would-be chute folded upward and poor brother hit the ground with a thud. The umbrella was totaled. We refolded it the best we could and placed it back in its holder. Maybe the driver wouldn't notice—so we hoped!

This story is supposed to be about a cap but I just had to

include the parachute jump. Three of us thought it amusing, one didn't. Monday rolled around and the Cat driver came in a truck with other workers. Water and fuel were put in the tractor and it was started up. With a big puff of smoke, away it went. As I stood watching the departure, a glistening object lying on the ground caught my attention. A closer view showed it to be the "big tank cap" from the Caterpillar. Holding the cap in my hand I took off in hot pursuit of tractor and driver. Running as hard as possible, I couldn't close the gap between us. My only hope of catching up would be if the tractor slowed down.

The Cat had reached a swampy area and was almost across when I arrived on the opposite side. What now? Surely this place was filled with poisonous reptiles. Fear began to overwhelm me—a decision had to be made. Casting caution aside and without breaking stride, into the mucky mire I plunged, running as fast as I could, tripping on roots, falling over logs and all the time hoping for no encounter with a snake. Reaching the other side, the tractor was just ahead. I yelled as loud as I could and the driver finally heard me and stopped. As I came up beside the tractor and held up the cap, the driver gave me a big grin. He even invited me to come up and ride with him a ways.

We soon came to a wagon road that would allow me to return home in relative safety. Thanking me again, the kindly workman handed me a shiny dime. A ride on a Caterpillar and a dime to boot, I'd made out like a bandit! Holding the coin in my hand ever so tightly, I excitedly began running once more, this time for home and to Mama. She would rejoice with me at my good fortune.

Reaching the edge of our property, I turned onto the long road that went by our house. About half way home I stopped to make sure my dime was still in my hand—I didn't feel it. Slowly I unfurled my fingers and the much-coveted coin fell into the loose sand at my feet. The reward of my labor seemed lost as it sank out of sight. The tears and sobs began immediately. Kneeling down I began carefully sifting the sand but could not find my treasure.

After hunting for some time, Floyd came on the scene. He suspected rightly that I had lost something in the sand and began to search as well. He found it in no time. He was told how I had acquired the dime, but now insisted it was his property because he found it. The argument continued as we reached the house. My mother, who was on the back porch churning, heard the ruckus and asked for an explanation. Upon hearing my story, she told Floyd to give me the dime. Angrily, Floyd hurled the coin out into the yard, a definite no-no with chickens about. The dime had not hit the ground when five or six hens darted for it. One old Rhode Island Red had it in her bill and was making for a patch of bamboo cane, the remaining chickens in swift pursuit, not to mention yours truly.

For a number of days I searched through the canes and the area around them. I am somewhat reluctant to say just what all I examined—I left no_unturned." Patience has its reward and I am happy to say, at last I found my long lost dime.

As a fun thing to do, my brothers and I would sit on the back porch and throw corn or small stones near the scratching chickens. Without fail they would head for the tossed objects. The successful hen would start running with it, the others chasing. Believe me, you would tire of the practice before the chickens did.

~ Grady Moody and Homebrew ~

Making homebrew and hard cider was a relatively common practice in Colonial Days. Most every year my Daddy made a beverage called homebrew. The drink was sometimes served to guests provided they were not teetotalers. At no time did I ever see my daddy tipsy from consuming this brew.

Neither my mother nor any of the children were permitted to drink this "delicious" stuff. After it had fermented properly, Kenneth would use a small hose to siphon it into bottles and jars. It was hard to see how Kenneth could fail to swallow some of it in the course of his work. The fact of the matter is we all eventually developed a liking for his joy-juice. When Daddy erected a good size building for syrup making, a large storage room was added to house the brew as well as the syrup. This room was kept under lock and key.

My two brothers assisted Daddy in the construction of the facility. In so doing they hinged one of the large planks in back of the storage compartment, thus providing them easy access to the homebrew. Once Daddy discovered the hinged plank, he promptly nailed it fast.

Grady Moody was a mulatto who lived about a mile and a half from us. Daddy would sometimes use Grady to drive our truck, or to plow. Floyd and I were quite fond of this dear man.

One day Daddy informed the family that we were going to town. This pleased us all. The wagon was hitched up and we were about to leave when Grady arrived to return a mower Daddy had borrowed from a distant neighbor. Even though going to town was one of our favorite things to do, when Floyd and I learned what Grady had come for, we asked if we could go with our friend rather than to town. Much to our surprise permission was granted. Maybe Daddy figured he could save a dime or two. If we had gone to town with him, we probably would have begged for a scoop of ice cream or a bag of boiled peanuts.

As soon as our folks were gone, Floyd asked Grady if he would like a bottle of Daddy's homebrew. Now Grady well knew that if my father found out that he had accepted the offer, his goose would be cooked. But the temptation proved too much for dear old Grady, so he allowed as how he ought to have a bottle of that good stuff.

Floyd, ingenious fellow that he was, soon had the lock off and produced not a bottle but a whole quart of Daddy's homebrew. Since it was not refrigerated, great care had to be exercised in handling it. Shake a bottle and it would blow the cap right off and about 95 percent of the contents would be lost. Removing the quart jar's lid could prove disastrous as well. Grady had sampled Daddy's makings before and knew just how to manage it.

The mule was hitched to the mower and we started for the Causey farm. Floyd was seated on the mule's back and Grady and I on the mower. It must have taken us an hour and a half to

reach the Causey place. After arriving, we promptly unhitched and began our return. The three of us were mounted on the mule, Floyd in front, Grady in the middle and me, precariously clinging to what was left of the rear. It was all I could do to keep from slipping off. I had to hold on to Grady for dear life.

You might think it an amusing sight to see three people riding on an old mule and I quite agree. However, it was not at all unusual in that day. Sometimes a family of four or five could be seen going down the road on a mule. Eventually we made it back home but before dismounting, I fell off! To make matters worse, she then stepped on my head. A gash, a big knot and some blood resulted. From this point on things become a little hazy. Grady most likely was wondering what Daddy's reactions would be. As for Floyd, I'm sure he knew exactly what he was going to tell our parents, *"That old mule kicked Raymond right in the head."*

~ Homebrew II ~

One eventful day Floyd and I were home alone. There were not many occasions when this happened. As pleasant as things were, restless spirits could find no contentment. The old saying "when the cat's away the mice will play" rings true. The adage was about to be confirmed again. One might say we were mischief—makers, Floyd and I. It's not like we wanted to be designated "trouble makers" but our joint activities always seemed to have negative connotations.

My brothers had found various ways to get into the storage shed and help themselves to the homebrew. This, of course, infuriated my daddy. He was determined that no one would ever again steal his brew and went to great lengths to secure the shed. To my brother Floyd, however, this fine day appeared to be a grand opportunity to once more partake of some of it. Floyd's cleverness was manifested at once. He got a crowbar and we climbed up onto the galvanized roof. At the ridge roll the crowbar was inserted under one of the tin sheets and pried up. I was left to hold the sheet back and keep a lookout for our father. Floyd descended into the shed and put three or four bottles in his pocket, handing one or two up to me. Things were working out just great!

As I held the sheet back, I looked up the road. *Then I saw him*, about two hundred yards away, walking, but coming fast. *"Floyd, it's Daddy!"* Floyd was out of the shed in less time than you could say "Jack Robinson." Pressing the galvanized sheets back in place and leaving the crowbar, we took off into a cornfield. As we ran we kept hoping Daddy didn't see us, and that the homebrew wouldn't explode in our pockets. Some distance out in the cornfield we stopped and began to dig a hole with our hands. We were putting the bottles in the hole when up walked Daddy. Red-handed is the word, *caught red-handed*!

Daddy marched us back to the house and into our bedroom. We were ordered to strip and lean over the bedstead, face down. Our posteriors would be the targets for what came next! Daddy produced his razor strop, (a long wide piece of leather) and began to flay away at our exposed parts. The beating we were getting was pure agony. Daddy was merciless. No amount of crying, pleading, begging or promising would cause him to stop his cruelty. I am convinced Daddy derived pleasure when we were being beaten.

He eventually stopped the whipping but only after his mad rage subsided. One thing I cannot understand about these occasions (and there were many): "why" was there no lecture afterwards?

Below are three questions I have asked and answered.

1. Did my father's discipline deter further negative behavior? The answer is NO.

2. Have I forgiven my father for his excessive punishment? Yes, most definitely.

3. Why do I disclose the naughty and sinful events of my childhood? Answer: So you may avoid similar behavior and yet know God can forgive sinners.

> *"Forgiving one another, even as God*
> *for Christ's sake has forgiven you.*
> – EPHESIANS 4:32

> *Children, obey your parents in the Lord,*
> *For this is right".*
> - EPHESIANS 6:1

School Days

~ Old Altamaha School ~

Appling County Georgia Altamaha School gets its name from a Creek Indian word that means "a dark and gloomy swamp." The Native Americans were referring to the bushes, vines, and trees that grew so thick along the banks of Georgia's largest river—the Altamaha River.

The school building was erected between 1906 and 1910. The last school term was 1934-1935. Some former teachers were Allie Myrtle Evans Land (my mother), Oxendine, W. R. Hardee, H. E. Brooks and Lois Hilton. The structure was never painted. It was torn down in the late 1970's.

Elsie Moss bought the old school and lot in 1935—sale price $100. The new Altamaha school's first classes began in January 1935 with Lois Hilton as principal. My three years at Altamaha had five-month terms.

"Baby Ruth had a little chick. Baby Ruth loved the little chick. The little chick loved Baby Ruth"—so reads the Young and Fields Literary Reader. The above quote is all I remember from my first grade textbook. A lot more learning experiences went on in our school than just reading, writing and arithmetic. It can best be described as *"life itself."*

The following series of mini stories are offered as proof of a "well rounded" education.

~ *The Spelling Bee* ~

A common practice of Georgia schools in the 1930's was the spelling bee. They were conducted every Friday and we students eagerly looked forward to them. The school had six grades in one room.

The teacher would begin the exercise by having the first graders come to the front, face the other students and align themselves in rows. The child nearest the teacher would be given a word from the "Swinton Word Book". If he or she spelled it correctly they remained standing, if not they returned to their seat. The "Bee" would continue until only one person was left—the winner. Due to the fact that a number of us were reasonably good spellers, this whole process took considerable time.

About the second round I began to develop a strong urge to—how shall I say it? Go potty? As time went on, my need did not subside but rather grew more and more intense. *Would this event never end?* I asked myself. Humiliation was staring me straight in the face! There was a definite need for some kind of plan. I was rapidly losing it. Becoming the laughing stock of the school was now a real possibility.

There comes a time in ones life when you just have to do what you gotta do. Plan A was to hold up my hand and when recognized by the teacher, ask to be excused—but she might deny my request. Plus, everyone would be looking at me and know I had a problem. There was nothing left for me to do but go to Plan B, which I immediately implemented. Standing as erect as possible and trying desperately to appear calm, I felt a warm satisfying sensation run down the leg of my overalls to my foot. It may be that you have had a similar experience, if so you know the joy of being relieved of a stressful situation.

When it was my turn to spell a word, I misspelled it and

promptly went to my seat. How blissful it was that my secret had not been discovered.

Some time elapsed before the teacher made her discovery. My countenance underwent a drastic change. What would she do? Search out the guilty one. Make us all swear to our innocence. As I pondered these things, our wonderful, thoughtful, gracious teacher took a piece of paper from her desk and in a most dignified manner, walked over to the scene of my recent distress, leaned down and with one quick swoop she removed from my sight all my potential embarrassment. It's possible only two people knew about this nerve-wracking experience, the teacher and me, oh yeah, you!

~ The Woods ~

One section of a forest that grew near our school was called "the woods." This area was thick with weeds, bushes, small shrubs, pines and a variety of other trees. Since the boys had not been provided with an outhouse, they would frequently retreat to the woods.

Much more than you might suspect went on in those woods. It was there the older boys came up with various forms of torture to inflict on the first and second graders. Things of a covert nature could be carried out with little chance of discovery.

In the woods a brave soul might have some "makings" to smoke. One could take a few puffs before passing the weed onto his buddies. A special treat was a big chaw of plug "tobacky" as we called it. Now I am not saying I participated in any of these activities, only that such doings were an everyday affair in the woods.

It would amaze you how well a boy could hide tobacco on

his person. My brother Floyd once sewed a small pocket inside the leg of his "long handles." If the teacher was told or witnessed that you had been smoking you could expect a severe flogging. Many times the teacher or our parents would ask to smell our breath if they suspected you of having smoked. However the woods provided the tobacco user with a "hide-saving" substance—the chlorophyll found in pine needles. Chewing pine needles freshened your breath and masked the tobacco odor. That place in the woods had real character; you could see it, taste it, touch it and definitely smell it!

~ The Sapling Shot ~

When a first or second grader visited the woods, he was usually met by a number of the older boys. They would ask him if he wanted to ride the sapling. Of course, his response was of no significance, he would be getting the ride whether he wanted it or not.

The heavier boys would climb up a young flexible pine tree, pulling it over towards the ground while others held the tree so it wouldn't spring back upright. Bringing the would-be rider over to the sapling, he would be instructed to grab hold near the tree's top and to wrap his legs around it as well. Once the rider was set, the boys in unison released their hold on the tree. There would be a "swoosh" as the sapling sprung upright and beyond. It was a terrific ride! But woe to anyone who did not have a firm grasp. The victim would be flung ten or fifteen feet out into who knows what?

There was risk of bodily injury, which occasionally happened, but most of the riders were thrilled with their experience and requested another shot.

~ Notched Switches ~

Corporal punishment of a student by a teacher these days is taboo—but it wasn't so in the 1930's. A teacher back then could give you the thrashing of your life. When you arrived home you could expect to receive another one, if a sibling told on you. I had three older brothers and they never failed to squeal.

One day another student and I did something that greatly annoyed our teacher and she angrily told us to remain in the room after the bell. When the bell rang, the other students scurried out the door. Their happy voices could be heard as they clumped down the front steps. I think not being able to go outside with the others was more distressing than the anticipated whipping. After a time, Miss Hilton told us to go to the woods and cut her some long switches.

My fellow sufferer and I arrived at the woods and were greeted by some of the other boys. They knew why we had come and offered their services. I had learned a long time ago to just agree with these fellows. One of the boys who had a knife proceeded to cut down four or five mean looking switches. Then, much to our surprise, he began to cut rings (or notches) about four or five inches apart on the switches.

We returned to the school and placed those instruments of torture on the teacher's desk, then took our seat. I was called to the front and told to bend over the desk. Miss Hilton selected one of the switches and drew it back over her shoulder. As she brought it forward the switch broke off a few inches above her hand. Picking the stick up once more she started the same procedure with the same results. Now it was clear she was not only angry, she was furious and frustrated. Attempting for a third and fourth time, the same thing happened. Grabbing the switches, she hurled them to the floor, shouting, "Get out, get out!" Then she sat down at her desk and began to cry. We were out of the door in a flash. There was always the possibility Miss Hilton would change her mind.

As a child I didn't understand the pressures many of the teachers were under. If I had, maybe I would have behaved better, maybe not.

The Woods

It's down to the woods I must go,
Don't ask why, I'm sure you know.

Linger not in the woods today,
"Tarry a while" some may say.

The voice in the woods, do not heed,
Flee that place with utmost speed.

So out of the woods I did fly,
Fast as one can bat the eye.

Many times into the woods I went.
Time I wish I had not spent.

No more to the woods as of yore,
For, there are no woods any more.

- BY RAY LAND

~ Accidents ~

One concern of parents while their children are at school is accidents. Thankfully most of today's schools have supervised activities and in some cases a nurse is on the premises. Teachers are trained in first aid, and paramedics, ambulances, doctors and hospitals are a phone call away. This was not the case in little one-room schools back in the early 1930's.

The school I attended had only one teacher. They received a teaching license by taking some training and passing a test. Salaries ranged from thirty to fifty dollars per month, and school terms were as low as 75 days.

In the three years I attended, skinned knees and elbows, bruises, black eyes, stubbed toes, splinters, bee stings, and burns from the potbelly heater etc. were common incidents. The usual treatment for such was washing, applying iodine and pouring turpentine or kerosene over the wound. I'll tell you about a few other accidents of a more serious nature.

39

~ Desk Carving ~

It seemed like some of the boys were determined to carve their name on their desktop. They managed to do it in spite of the constant scrutiny of the teacher.

One day a class was involved in some kind of exercise at the front of the room. Suddenly a loud scream came from the back and then more screams by some of the girls. The teacher rushed to the disturbance to find an older boy bleeding profusely. He was in the process of carving his name when the knife slipped off the desk and went deeply into his right thigh. With every heartbeat you could see the blood being pumped out onto the floor. We all stood around staring. No one made a move to do anything. The fact is, none of us knew what to do.

Finally we were instructed to go and collect spider webs and bring them to the teacher. The children ran out of the school and took off in every direction. Quite a number were crawling up under the school and some girls went to their outhouse. Most of us were out in the woods looking around old burnt out stumps and alongside fallen trees. None of us were too successful in finding webs.

One by one we returned to the school with our finds. The teacher was busy placing the webs over the stab wound. Surprisingly the bleeding had almost subsided. After a few more minutes it ceased to bleed. The boy who had stabbed himself eventually went home. He was one of the older students. Try as I might I can't remember if he ever returned to school. I think his father just put him to work in the fields. No doubt the spider web treatment was an old home remedy. Did it stop the flow of blood? It certainly appeared to. God is very merciful.

~ Knocked Out ~

The glass in the cloakroom window had all been knocked out. For some reason, which I am hard pressed to explain, climbing up into the opening appealed to me. Needless to say it was the wrong thing to do and quite dangerous. People would notice me and that seemed terribly important to me at the time. It would be a struggle to get up there, but surely it would be worth it.

As I stood there in the window and gazed into the schoolyard I saw the children looking at me. My moment in the sun was all so thrilling. WOW! Being way up high above my fellow students gave me star status!

Suddenly there was a cracking noise and the entire frame began to come out of the building, with me holding on to it for dear life! Down, down we went to the ground below, hitting it and making a loud thud—I was knocked out! When I came to, I was surrounded by a multitude of faces, all peering down at the idiot on the ground. By the way, *live and learn*".

"Man's pride shall bring him low".
- PROVERBS 29:23

~ Caring, Compassionate Kenneth ~

My brother Floyd told me this story. One day a little girl was happily running around in the schoolyard playing with her classmates when she suddenly began to scream and cry. A huge splinter of wood had pierced her foot. It had gone in the bottom and protruded out the top.

As the children gathered around, their faces mirrored deep concern and compassion for their poor little classmate. The

41

teacher was present but had no answer for this serious problem. With no phones, no doctors, or nearby neighbors with a car to take her to the hospital which was in Baxley ten or twelve miles away, it was a desperate situation.

While we were pondering our dilemma, my brother Kenneth made his way to where the precious little girl lay. Reaching down he picked her up in his arms, made his way through the crowd, climbed up and down the stile, and started off down the road. The Hutto farm was two miles away and Mr. Hutto had an automobile. I can just see him, as he carried the little victim to a place where she could receive help.

"Do unto others as you would have them do unto you."
- MATTHEW 7:12

~ *The "Seven Year Itch"* ~

Scabies was known in my school days as the dreaded "seven year itch." The itch didn't bug me as much as the medicine that was used to treat it—it smelled so awful the odor made you want to barf. A tiny little itch mite would bore in under your skin and cause you to scratch like crazy. It wasn't just one of those critters that attacked you, there must have been "zillions."

It was assumed by many that children who did not bathe would most likely be host to the mites. My mother was an extremely sanitary person and insisted that her boys keep themselves clean. There was lots of contact between the students of the little one room school, so getting the "itch" was pretty much a certainty. Sometimes children would remain home for a few days. They were treated with a kind of sulfur solution that made their skin look yellow, and that smelled like rotten eggs. By the way, it didn't really last seven years.

~ Baseball ~

At Altamaha school we played a variety of playground games such as marbles, tops, drop the handkerchief, tag, leap frog, hopscotch, and America's favorite, baseball.

Babe Ruth was a name familiar to most of us, and he was our hero. We liked to pretend that "we" were the famous Athlete. It was strange how this man could impact some of us. We had no radios, no television and rarely did we see a newspaper, let alone read it. Yet, amazingly, Babe Ruth seemed to be a household word in our community.

Boys played the game according to the rules of the day although there were notable differences, if compared to present day contests. There were no uniforms, no gloves and no shoes. Our bats and balls were all made by one or more of the players.

To make a bat: First you cut down a Hickory sapling with the right diameter. Then you cut it to the correct length. The bark was peeled off and the bat was scraped with a knife. This completed the final step in producing an "Altamaha Slugger." Our baseball was made by tightly wrapping string around a small sponge rubber ball until the desired size was obtained. The string's loose end was tucked under some of the wraps and tied off.

"Play ball" the teacher might shout! And that we did, with energy and enthusiasm! The game had exciting moments. When a batter hit the ball exceptionally hard, it would cause the string to unwind. By the time it reached the outfield there was little left to catch. Stopping the game, the ball was wrapped again, and play resumed.

Occasionally older boys would play another school. Their opponents' equipment was the same as our own, so if someone showed up with a glove, we cried, "foul."

The Great Depression was a tough time in which to live. Parents could ill afford to buy children athletic gear. Putting food on the table was their prime objective. We simply made do as well as we could. There certainly were no hundred-dollar gym shoes, just some thick calloused feet. But I dare say the children of my day were more contented than today's youth. Most of us were poor but that was no disgrace.

I once heard a story about a very sad king who asked his advisers how he might become happy. He was told he would have to wear the shirt of the happiest man in his realm. A search was made in the kingdom until the individual was found. An anxious king went out into the countryside to meet him. "My good man" the king said, "may I wear your shirt?" "I'm sorry sire, I have no shirt," the happy soul replied.

"...Having food and raiment let us therewith be content."
- 1 TIMOTHY 6:8

~ *Dinner Buckets* ~

To rural southerners in the 1930's, dinner was the noon-time meal—"lunch" was not in our vocabulary. We carried our food to school in a shiny one-gallon syrup bucket. Since our noon meal was in this container, we called it a "dinner bucket". The vessel looked much like a "paint can". A tight fitting lid kept the flies and ants away from your food. Siblings shared the same bucket.

Ordinarily the pails would be placed on a shelf in the cloakroom, or sometimes we would find a cool shady spot and tie them to low hanging branches. How did we identify our own bucket? A very good question! Occasionally there would be bucket thefts, and generally it was the school bullies who would take your dinner. When caught, they would insist it was theirs because the buckets all looked the same.

So, what was inside our buckets? Depending on the circumstances of our family, we might find a variety of goodies. The number one item was probably a slab or slice of fried grits. There might be a syrup filled biscuit, a fried piece of good old hickory smoked ham, a boiled egg, a baked sweet potato and Mama might include a big piece of gingerbread. All the above was pretty much standard fare but you certainly didn't get all the items at once! For some it might be just some grits and a biscuit.

"...Giving thanks always for all things."
- EPHESIANS 5:20

~ *First Moving Picture Show* ~

One day our teacher stunned us by announcing that a moving picture would be shown in our school. We'd heard of such stars as Buck Jones and Tom Mix but none of us had ever seen an actual film. This tremendous event would take place in a couple of days. The admission price would be ten cents per child. In the event you could not scrape up a dime, the show's promoter would accept ten fresh eggs as entry fee.

Young minds began immediately to think of ways to persuade reluctant parents to cough up a dime—as the saying goes "money was as scarce as hen's teeth". Somehow we managed to obtain the money.

The big night finally came and my brothers and I were off to see the grand extravaganza. We arrived at the school in plenty of time. No way were we going to be late for our first moving picture show. Workers were busy putting sheets over the windows and setting the projector in place on the teacher's desk. A sheet hanging on the back wall would serve as a makeshift screen.

We had been told the action would start at dusk and we were all anxiously awaiting the moment. The audience was largely children, their eyes bulging out and their mouths agape. If there was ever an excited group of boys and girls, this was it. A room full of assorted odors and very little oxygen, plus being extremely hot, did not seem to bother us.

Suddenly a whir and clicking sounds were heard. A flickering bright light appeared on the hanging sheet, followed by lots of letters or words that I could not read. *Then it happened*! There on the hanging sheet on our schoolhouse wall were COWBOYS, cowboy hats, guns, horses, and our big handsome hero with a giant white hat! Bank robbers. More shooting. A beautiful girl kidnapped. The hideout. Blazing guns. Outlaws captured. Our hero and beautiful girl ride off into the sunset—finis!

We had just experienced a most marvelous thing. Something new and frightening, yet exciting beyond words. That night on the way home, my brothers and I talked and talked about this memorable event—and we discussed it for many days afterward. Let me see; was it dimes and eggs or all eggs? *Maybe just dimes...hmm*?

~ The New Outhouse ~

We began the 1933-1934-school season on an optimistic note. Things at Altamaha were looking up. The trustees provided us with a brand new outhouse, a "two holer".. No more trips to the woods to respond to nature's beckoning. Now there would be privacy and comfort. The new edifice let us think someone had our best interest at heart.

A young lad was about to enter the new facility when he let out a horrific scream! A number of us were playing nearby and rushed over to ascertain the reason for such a loud outburst. The screamer pointed to the side of our new outhouse

and said just one word, "Snake!" About two feet of the reptile was visible. It was a big one.

The commotion attracted the teacher's attention, prompting him to mosey over for a look. There was no floor in the new outhouse. We boys stood perplexed. Mr. Brooks, desiring to show his courage and skill, reached down and yanked the reptile out! He began swinging him around and around over his head. Suddenly, he gave the snake a quick snap, off came the head "clean as a whistle." We stood staring—this teacher was really something.

Incidentally, the snake was a coach whip. It got its name from the horsewhips found on buggies and coaches. Some said the coach whip would wrap itself around a victim and beat it to death and I can tell you there was not one boy in Altamaha School who didn't believe it. Our new outhouse was great, but someone ought to put a floor in it, don't you think?

~ The Five Mile Tale ~

Did your grandparents ever tell you how far they had to walk to school? Was it three miles or five miles? Now I won't dispute any claims because they may be accurate. What I will say is sometimes old tales get stretched. I would often tell my children about my long three to five mile walks. "Did you really walk five miles Daddy?" Questions like that caused me to wonder just how far it was to a couple of places. I needed to verify those distances.

Thanks to my sister Faye, I was given the opportunity to see for myself. She drove me down to the old home place in South Georgia in March 2003. I had estimated that the mailbox was approximately three miles away. My sister and I drove the distance in her big white "Caddy." It checked out at a disappointing 1.2 miles. I was certain it would be more than that. Well, at least my guess will be right about the school. Three to five miles for sure! Again I was wrong, would you believe it was only 1.6 miles?

What ever made me think the school and mailbox were so much farther away? After some thought, obvious reasons came to mind. When you are a child, distance seems much longer than for an adult. I was simply remembering the walk as a child would remember it.

A country boy on his way to school or the mailbox would be interested in many things. For instance, he might climb a tree to peek into a bird's nest or pick a few wild plums or berries. Then there would be a nice sandy ditch, and boys liked to walk in sandy ditches. A snake crossing the road would get plenty of attention. There was a shallow stream that crossed the road, which we called a ford. Wading around in the cool refreshing water was an absolute must. Throwing a few flat skipper stones across the glistening water would be expected from any normal boy. Pulling down wild grape vines was great fun, especially if there happened to be ripe grapes on the vines. Rabbits and birds would occupy us for a short time, as did a great many other things.

Maybe your grandparents did walk five miles to school. If they walked along an old country road where the homes were few and far apart, where the smell and beauty of nature might distract them from their objective, causing wandering feet to go here and there, then I know it was five miles to school. I know—I walked it. Never mind what the odometer in Faye's big white "Caddy" read.

~ Bad Boys and Slingshots ~

Not many of the boys who attended school wanted to be there. They were country boys who loved to roam the woods searching for wild grapes, blackberries and plums to satisfy their sweet tooth. Dashing off to the old swimming hole to cool their hot sweaty bodies was extremely gratifying. Six hours in one room, listening to a lot of meaningless words was not our cup of tea. We were sure it was a waste of time. Because of such discontent, many boys did poorly academically. Mischief and unrest was the sad result. The teachers' attempts at keeping order were often quite futile

Slingshots were part of every boy's arsenal. They were usually well made and powerful enough to kill small game like rabbits and squirrels, not to mention snakes. Unhappily, little birds were the most frequent victims of this lethal weapon. Savage slingshot battles were fought by rival groups of boys, oft-times resulting in serious injury.

Most parents strenuously objected to their children having slingshots, including my mother who was dead set against them. My older brothers made them anyway, but kept them hidden from our parents. Brother Cecil was a very accurate shooter. When school was not in session, boys would shoot all of the school's windowpanes out. Entering the school, they would proceed to break the hinged seats apart to obtain a few ball bearings. These would be used as marbles or ammo for their slingshots. Although this destructive activity was an annual event, no one was ever apprehended. Serious consequences would have resulted if the boys had been caught. I witnessed these senseless acts on at least one occasion.

Bad boys? I'm pretty sure you will agree that they were. Did I participate? What do you think?

Farm Work

God has ordained that man should toil to provide food for himself and his household. We learn from the account of man's fall in the Garden of Eden that labor is a divinely appointed duty to be faithfully carried out.

During the Great Depression, money to buy necessities was in short supply for the small farm owner. Any farm with less than 200 acres might well be considered small. Cotton, the money crop, was sold for five cents a pound in 1932. "Five cent cotton and forty cent meat, how in the world is the poor man going to eat?"- So a popular song of the day proclaimed.

There was one thing that could be found on our farm in great abundance, of that you could be absolutely sure. It was work and more work! Often before the sun came up, we would be busy with our chores—fourteen-hour workdays were not uncommon.

"In the sweat of your face shall you eat bread".
- GENESIS 3:19

~ The Sled ~

The sled was a primitive but practical multipurpose vehicle, and could be found on most South Georgia farms in the 1930's. It was inexpensive to make, and was designed to be pulled by a mule to go between plant rows.

Most of the needed materials could be found in the farmer's scrap lumber pile. Two runners, a floor, frame sides covered with croker sacks, and you would have a sled. The runners were tapered up at the front to cut down on drag and could be pulled with ease. Floyd loved driving the sled. I did too when the opportunity presented itself. It was great fun to ride between the rows of corn or down to the watermelon patch. Unless there was a fun aspect to it, I never liked to work. My Daddy had two nicknames for me. One was "Sammy", the other "Lazy Bones".

~ Oh, Those Dreaded Chores ~

Carrying Water: Water was brought out into the field to the workers in an eight or ten quart galvanized bucket. A dipper was supplied. Several trips had to be made during the course of the day.

Chopping Cotton: Of all my duties, this was the most objectionable. A hoe was used to chop away cotton plants when they were too thick. Then dirt was pulled up around the young plants. We removed the weeds as well.

Churning: Milk and cream were poured into an earthen crock or container. A protruding long handled plunger was placed in the churn. A lid with a center hole went down over the handle and sealed the churn. We plunged up and down, up and down until we ultimately got butter.

Cropping Tobacco: Farmers did not want their tobacco plants to bloom. Our job was to snip the buds off before blossoming. This was so all the energy of the plant would go into the leaves.

Cutting Kindling: I was not permitted to use an axe and perform this function until I was eight years old. Rich, red-looking pine tar sections were found in some pine tree logs. This wood was cut out of the log and into smaller pieces called kindling, which burns rapidly and was used to start fires in stoves and fireplaces.

Digging Manure: This was the most demeaning, disgusting and dirty duty done by dear old Daddy, and I dreaded helping him! Mules and cows would be let out of their stables to go into an enclosed area called the paddock. Over a period of time, some mighty potent fertilizer was built up—several inches of the stuff. We would shovel it into the wagon, take it out to the fields and scatter it. You might say we were recycling.

Drawing Water: The well we used for drinking water was at the end of our kitchen porch. Across the road in the paddock was a watering trough and a second well for the animals. The water was crystal clear and very cool. The trough was filled on a daily basis.

Feeding Animals: The farmer's livestock was most vital to him and his household. Keeping the animals well fed was extremely important. At times I would be called on to do the feeding.

Cows provided us with fresh milk from which butter was made. The bovine was fed ground corn, hay and fodder. During the day the cows grazed in the pasture.

Mules did all of the really hard work on the farm. Their diet consisted of dry corn on the cob, hay and fodder.

Pigs and hogs ate about anything and wound up being eaten. Grunting and snorting, they ate peelings, rinds, table scraps, leftovers, rotten melons, a pulpy like weed we called "clover", and even the dishwater from the slop bucket. Oh, how I liked to watch porky eat!

Chickens were fed a mash of ground corn and other seeds. Our chickens were not confined and could scavenge during the day.

Dogs ate mostly table scraps. These animals were not kept as pets but were used for hunting, and as watchdogs—although there was a bond between our dogs and the family.

Feeding Sugar Cane Mill: Sugar cane would be brought to the mill and stacked. Individual pieces were run through the rollers, which squeezed the juice out into a barrel. This was another tiring job, complicated by swarming sugar-loving bees.

Irish and Sweet Potatoes: We raised large amounts of Irish and sweet potatoes. The Irish potatoes were dug out by hand. Sweet potatoes were plowed up and then harvested while on your knees. It's a wonder I enjoyed eating them but I did and still do.

Husking Corn: Just when you thought you would have some free time, Daddy would send Floyd and me to the barn to husk corn, or as we would say, "shuck corn." It was usually cold and our hands would be raw and red from trying to remove the husks. This was one tough job for a seven year old!

Killing Potato Beetles: These pests seemed to multiply faster than we could kill them. They hatched from clusters of eggs laid on the underside of the leaves. The larva was a plump little red thing that made me sick just to look at it. Amazingly, this larva would transform itself into a sleek looking beetle, with off-white and black stripes. It was easily identified as the Colorado potato beetle. We knew of a gardener who responded to a magazine ad that offered a "guaranteed potato beetle killer". The price? A mere three dollars. The money was sent in immediately and the gardener anxiously awaited his purchase. When it came, he opened the package and removed two wooden blocks and a sheet of instructions. This is what he read, "Place beetle on Block A, bring Block B down forcefully onto Block A. *This action is guaranteed to kill the beetle*!

Loading Wood, and Scorpions: We took the mule and wagon into the woods to look for firewood before the winter set in. Once we located a dead pine tree, it was sawed into roughly three foot pieces. The pine bark was usually loose and we would carefully pull it off. All kinds of bugs would be found between the bark and the log's main body. Our caution was not without good reason as something sinister and dreadful was often found behind that bark—scorpions! This creature could inflict a nasty sting. If several of the really large ones stung you, their poison might prove fatal. Gathering and loading wood required a watchful eye.

Mending Fences: Repairing the pasture fences was another cold weather project. Cows rubbing against the post would loosen them and cause the barbed wire to become slack. A sledgehammer, nails, and tamping sticks were brought along. Small stones and dirt were put around the post at ground level and tramped down. A stick was put around the wire and twisted—this removed the slack. Daddy was a competent sixty-five year old and I was but seven.

~ Picking and Picking ~

Blackberries were my favorite things to pick, probably because I could eat all I wanted! This delicious berry grew in abundance on our farm. We would fill washtubs with them. Mama would "put up" (can) dozens of jars of the berries and made lots of jam and jelly as well. A blackberry pie could be made any time of the year. Jam and jelly with hot biscuits and butter was a special breakfast treat.

Peas were a big part of our diet. We picked black-eyed peas, English peas and field peas. We also picked peaches, pecans, butter beans and other assorted vegetables. Not too unpleasant, but still work.

Cotton is now picked with a machine, but for around two

hundred years it was done by hand. We have described else-where, in some detail, the physical demands of cotton picking especially when the sun was scorching hot.

~ Planting Tobacco ~

Tobacco beds were formed by laying logs end-to-end form-ing a large rectangular plot. The soil inside the enclosure was a rich, loose, dark loam. Brush was burned on top of the soil to produce ash and perhaps destroy seeds from weeds. The bed would be raked to smooth the surface, and the tobacco seed was sown. Cheesecloth was stretched over the bed to keep birds and animals out. The cloth created a kind of greenhouse effect. In no time thousands of plants would be popping up.

The field that was to receive the plants was prepared. Young vigorous seedlings were removed from the bed, placed in a container and kept moist. A rather strange looking object was used to facilitate the planting. I'll do my best to describe it. It was a three-foot long metal cylinder six or seven inches wide, tapered to a point on one end with a small opening. The other end of the cylinder was open with a handle across the top. The pointed end had a spring-loaded valve. A wire ran from the valve to a ring located just under the handle. Gripping the handle and pulling on the ring with the forefinger opened the valve. The main cylinder body would be filled with water and kept in an upright position.

Starting at the end of a row, the "hole maker" was pushed into the soil, withdrawn, and a small amount of water was released into the hole. Additional holes would be made, and so on. A second person would be employed to keep the water compartment filled. A third would remove plants from a flat or bucket and place them in the hole. A fourth person kept the planter supplied with plants.

The final step in this process was to fill or push dirt around the plant while holding it upright. This happened to be my responsibility. As you may note, we employed five people, six if necessary. When everything was set, we all headed out to the field. The plan was to do about ten acres. Tomorrow, maybe the same—we'll wait and see about that.

~ Raising Tobacco (detailed) ~

Tobacco was a money crop. We raised it solely to produce revenue. Unlike cotton, tobacco required a great deal of attention. So why not plant all cotton? Since the farmer could not predict what cotton might sell for, he planted two money crops, hoping at least one of them would bring some money. Below is a list of functions necessary to produce tobacco for marketing:

- Prepare "large beds" for planting seedlings.
- Prepare field to receive young plants.
- Plant
- Water
- Plow, cultivate and weed.
- Remove and destroy tobacco worms by hand.
- Remove the suckers growing between leaves and stem by hand.
- Top and snip before blooming.
- Crop (pull) the leaves off for curing. Place leaves on sled and deliver to tobacco barn.
- Tie leaves onto a six-foot stick.
- Place tobacco on racks inside the barn for curing.

(Note: The tobacco barn was about two stories high.
Racks ran from near the ceiling to about five feet
off the floor. The racks were long poles with upright
supports. The poles went from side to side. At least
three people were needed to attach the tobacco onto
the poles.

♦ A Stoker (furnace attendant) would have to maintain a constant temperature for many hours.
Stokers would work in shifts around the clock.
Note: The furnace was built through the tobacco
barn's wall. Inside, flues ran around the barn's
perimeter.

♦ Piles of wood must be on hand to keep fires
burning.

♦ Remove cured tobacco.

♦ Sort the tobacco into huge baskets.

♦ Transport to warehouse for auction.

The above list is basic. Knowing when to plant, to pick and
to sell were also critically important decisions.

～ More Farm Chores ～

Pulling Clover: Late in the day Floyd hitched the mule to
the sled and headed out to the cornfield. Most of the time
I would accompany him. We were in search of an unusual
weed we called clover. There are over 300 kinds of clover but
the particular variety we searched for bore little resemblance
to what most of us think of as clover today. Growing in soft
soil among the corn, the plant is easily uprooted. We filled
the sled in a short time. Once we had a load, it was off to the
pigpen. Throwing the clover into the hog trough, the "oink-

ers" would begin devouring it as if they were starving. Pulling clover and feeding it to the pigs was really a fun thing to do!

Pulling Weeds: Pulling weeds or "weeding" never had much appeal for me but the choice of whether I did or didn't do it was never my decision to make. When you are ordered to do something, the fun, if there was any, was taken right out of it.

Shooing Flies: None of our doors or windows had screens. Birds, bats, bugs, bees and flies could come in and out as they pleased. The most annoying nuisance was the pesky fly. This noxious insect seemed to challenge would-be swatters, flying away just in the nick of time.

When company came to Sunday dinner, so did the flies. Our old bugaboo was not invited and definitely not welcome. This would be an occasion to bring out our best defensive weapon, the "shoo fly fan". I don't remember the real name of this fan, so I called it the "shoo-fly fan"—it does seem to be appropriate, don't you think?

To make one of these fans: First, cut yourself a round stiff stick about six feet in length, and one half inch in diameter. Next, you will need four or five sheets of newspaper, opened up and laid flat. Now mix a cup of water and flour paste. Apply a six-inch swath of paste down the center of the top sheet. Place stick on center of pasted strip. Make sure one end of stick is even with top edge of sheet. Fold sheet over top of stick. Press paper down and allow it to dry. Repeat the pasting and folding process one sheet at a time. When all sheets are dry, one step remains. Start at the open edges of the sheets and cut one-inch strips to within three inches of the stick.

Congratulations, you have now made a "shoo fly fan". Wasn't that fun? Now here comes the work part. Your guests take their seats at the table. Mama hands you the "fan" and directs you to stand behind the visitors. The food is brought in and placed on the table. You immediately begin waving the fan back and forth. The idea is to prevent the unwanted pest from landing on the food. A good shoo fly waver person might keep those flies airborne for the entire meal.

The negative side of this operation will soon become apparent. Your arms begin to grow tired, and you see the guests gobbling up all the food. *"There goes the last chicken leg and now the banana pudding has vanished. Nothing is going to be left for us to eat." NOT FAIR!*

Shucking 'n Shelling: The heading to this farm work episode has a nice ring to it, don't you agree? It sounds as if the task is a pleasant one. I wish I could tell you it was, but it wasn't! After the crops were harvested you might think we could all kind of sit back and relax a bit; but you would be oh so wrong! My Daddy could find work to do anytime of day or night.

Floyd and I would be sent to the corn storage to shuck and shell corn. One look inside the corncrib was shocking! There was a mountain of corn in that place. Most of the time, Daddy wanted a specific amount of shelled corn. We would remove the husks from a considerable number of ears and begin shelling.

The corn sheller is rather difficult to describe. It was about waist high and had four legs. There was a funnel like opening to an enclosed disk. The disk was covered with spikes and connected to a handle on the outside of the Sheller. Pushing the ear of corn into the opening and turning the handle caused the ear to rotate. This action and contact with the disk's spikes removed the grains of corn from the cob. A sack or bucket underneath the Sheller caught the shelled corn. Cobs were saved for a compost pile. If you remained at this job for several hours, your hands would become very sore. Removing husks from dry ears of corn was not easy.

Stripping Fodder: After harvesting the corn another valuable food would come from the corn stalk.—fodder. The stalk's leaves were stripped off, made into a bundle and pushed down over the remaining stalk. Later this fodder would be taken to the barn to be fed to the livestock.

Straightening Nails: If you have ever observed a carpenter at work, you will notice he rarely picks up a dropped nail and never a bent one. The time consumed in retrieving a dropped nail is worth more than the nail itself. My Daddy was from the old school—you saved everything. Bent, blunted and rusty nails were thrown in a bucket to be used again. One work assignment I disliked so intensely was to straighten those old nails. Placing a bent one on the anvil and pounding it with the hammer until reasonably straight was no easy matter. I think there were more smashed fingers than straight nails.

Yard Sweeping: Not a single home in our community had a grass lawn. The area around our house was completely barren. Possible reasons for this were that no one had lawn mowers, snakes could be easily spotted, and where will the chickens scratch? (Just kidding) So here is this humongous sea of sand and soil and it had to be swept. Mama usually did the job but sometimes it became my lot or my brothers'. We made our own brush brooms. Short, slender brush was tied around a longer piece that served as a handle. This broom, made of broom sage, was ideal for sweeping the yard.

~ Turning 'n Turning ~

They stood silently in the shed. A passerby would pay little or no heed to them. Nothing about the two devices would arouse any degree of curiosity or wonder. BUT should we boys see Daddy drag one of them out to the shade of the big oak tree, we would quickly disappear—or try to! Daddy usually nabbed one of us before we could escape.

What was it about these devices that evoked such fear and dread in the Land brothers? W-O-R-K! Turning the handle of the whetstone for perhaps an hour was sheer torture. It had to be turned at a fast rate. If you slowed down you might receive a crack over the head with whatever Daddy was endeavoring to sharpen. It just could be that those inevitable "noggin" clunks were responsible for my loathing for the grindstone.

Turning the blower for the forge was considerably easier than turning the grindstone. Being a mere child, it was hard to focus on anything for a long period. At least I would receive fewer knots on my head turning the blower.

Fun Times

"All work and no play makes Jack a dull boy" so the old saying goes. Thankfully we found some fun things to do. The first three described here were indeed "fun" but were also extremely dangerous. They never met with our parent's approval.

~ *The Flying Jenny* ~

Compared to today's amusement park rides, the "flying jenny" was "dullsville". It wasn't the ride itself that caused our parents concern. Serious injury could occur, even death. My ingenious and mischievous older brothers constructed the potentially lethal "jenny". A tree was sawed down about three feet above the ground. A hole was drilled into the center of the stump and a steel rod was driven into it leaving approximately six inches protruding. Axle grease was placed around the rod and stump top. Then a heavy plank with a hole drilled in its center was placed over the rod.

The "jenny" looked very much like a seesaw but instead of going up and down it went round and round. Someone would stand near the center and push on the plank. The pusher had to "duck down" as the riders flew around. The "flying jenny" was an exciting ride but woe to the person who let go of the plank—and woe to the pusher if he raised his head before the plank and riders slowed down. All of this excitement was short-lived. Daddy soon discovered our merry maker and dismantled it immediately. But the fun we had on the "jenny" was well worth the effort we put into building it.

~ Riding the Cows ~

Even though Daddy absolutely forbade us to ride the cows we did it anyway. In fact cow riding was one of our favorite pastimes. This sport required a certain amount of skill, which could only be learned by experience. If Daddy caught us doing it the penalty for disobedience would be severe.

My first experience was disastrous. The brothers were riding a young cow (heifer) in front of our house. It appeared to be great fun and easy to do. I begged them to let me have a go at it. They readily consented. Their quick response to my request should have served as a warning to me—these boys were not big on sharing their amusement. One of them picked me up and set me up near the shoulders of the bovine. There was a loud SWAT and laughter as the heifer took off like a rocket! This was all too new to me, so I was at a loss as to what to do. Jumping off didn't seem to be an option but staying on the cow's back was becoming impossible. The animal ran wildly down a slight slope toward a swamp, the same swamp from which a big rattler had emerged. I was leaning forward trying to put my arms around her neck and somehow hold on. As we entered the mucky bog, the cow began to slow down. I was determined to stay on her. No way did I want to fall into that snaky mire.

By the time we came to a stop, the heifer was up to her knees in black muck. My feet and arms were around the cows' neck and I was looking up into her slobbery face. Fear gripped me as I thought of the cottonmouths and rattlers that surely abounded in that swamp. I wasn't about to let go of my hold, slobber or no slobber. My brothers thought it was hilarious. I *didn't!*

~ The "Kar Tar" ~

If you are wondering just what a "kar tar" is, I'm pleased to enlighten you. It is simply a car tire. Southern Georgia farm folks with their strong rural accent would pronounce it "kar tar". An old tire was extremely popular as a plaything in my youth. We would roll it around in the yard and up and down the road. Hours would be spent pretending we were driving a truck or car. Reflecting back on bygone days, we remember the joyful times we had "just imagining".

What possible harm could come from pushing that old "kar tar" around? Where was the danger? It might be a month or

more before a car would pass our home, so we were not likely to be run over by an automobile. But my brothers were not content with just rolling an old tire around. They somehow had to make it more exciting. One of them finally came up with a bright idea and I was to play a big part in this new tire-rolling concept. One brother would hold the tire upright, the other two would pull the sidewalls out as wide as they could. Now guess who would sit inside the tire? Forming a kind of triangle, my brothers would roll me from one to another. Everyone, including myself, thought this was great fun. All went well for a time. Then one day as my mother was raking and burning leaves, another brainstorm was hatched. They would roll me through the fire. *Imagine!* Without consulting yours truly, they began rolling the tire directly at the huge pile of smoking and burning leaves. My mother looked up in horror as she saw the approaching tire but could not stop it. *Into the flaming inferno I went!* And what do you think happened? Thanks to a merciful God, I came out of that pile without even a hair being singed.

My dear mother reacted as any responsible parent should. The boys received a lecture and were ordered to never place me inside that "kar tar again". Needless to say, after this hair-raising experience, I never *wanted* another ride. Those brothers of mine just *could not be trusted.*

~ Games ~

Hellover: This particular game has a variety of other names. It is called "easy over", "evee ivy over", "ante over", etc. After I tell you how it is played you'll likely say, "Oh, we called it such and such." "Easy over" can be played with two or more players, though it is more fun if a large number of boys and girls participate. Sides are chosen and positioned on opposite sides of the house. A soft sponge ball, about the size of a baseball, is tossed over the house as our side yelled loudly, "Hellover". Once the ball was tossed, we waited quietly. Should someone from the other side catch the ball, they would all run over to our side of the house. When this began to occur, we would start to run to the side our opponents had vacated. The person with the ball would attempt to hit somebody by throwing it at him. Since we did not know who had the ball, we were leery of anyone we encountered. If you made it back to the opposite side without being struck, you were safe. Those hit by the ball were eliminated. Play continued until no opponents remained.

There were some variations to playing the game, but the rules were clarified before starting the game. If you were a boy you could expect to get "clobbered good" by the one who caught the ball. The cute little girls would be merely touched. After all, we were southern gentlemen!

Marbles: Marbles was one of my favorite games even though I never excelled at it. My brothers would always beat me but this did not dampen my enthusiasm for the game. My brother Cecil was a fantastic player. He could knock a marble out of a ten-foot circle with ease. Our Mama did not want us to play "for keeps." She allowed as to how that was gambling! But Cecil's pockets would be bulging with his winnings. If you were caught playing "for keeps" on the school playground, you were in big trouble. A teacher would about wear the seat of your pants out with a switch—Ouch!

Have you ever heard the expression "knuckle down"? It comes from the game of marbles. The shooter must have at least one knuckle touching the ground when the marble leaves his hand.

There are many kinds of marble games. My favorite one involved a lag line and four holes. First, second, third, and the granny hole. You really want to know how this marble game was played? Send me a dollar and a self-addressed...just kidding!

Ancient Roman and Egyptian children played marbles before the Lord Jesus was born.

Washers: This is a fun game. All you need is eight very large washers –four painted one color and four another color. You will need two wide but shallow empty cans. Make sure the washers will fit into the cans. Clear two non-grassy areas, about twenty or more feet apart. Sink the cans in holes, approximately two and one half inches below the ground level. Taper the dirt down to the top of the can. Score one point for each washer tossed into the can. Stand behind one can when throwing to the other can. Alternate tosses. This game is for two players. No points are scored when an opponent's washer tops yours. A 2½-inch washer is best for throwing. Hardware stores carry them. Believe me, you will have great fun!

Tag and Hide-n-Seek: These two games are surely well known to all.

Swinging: Who has not played on a swing? Most of us have at one time or another. In our back yard we had a rope tied to a limb high up in a big oak tree. The ropes' loose end was secured to an old tire. You may have seen this type of swing or even played on one. Because the rope was so long, you could travel a good distance and reach a great height. My siblings and I had a fantastic time on our swing. There was need of caution however. Should you push the swinger out from the tree, he could be seriously injured or killed.

One day my pusher decided to amuse himself by pushing me out and away from the tree's trunk. This was a very bad thing to do! As the tire swung back, I struck the tree with considerable force and my injury was quite severe.

Daddy witnessed the accident and promptly ordered the swing to be taken down. My brother's foolishness had ruined it for all. There would be no more fun playing on our swing.

Wading in the Creek: Wading in the cool creek was a delightful thing to do, especially on a scorching hot day. I did most of my wading in fords. A ford was where the road crossed the creek. The water would seldom be more than a foot deep and maybe fifteen feet wide. My brother Floyd and I would run for a mile to enjoy wading in a cool stream. Sitting down in the water with our clothes on was refreshing. Ahh, nice!

Owl Hunting: There was something haunting and mysterious about the wise old owl. Actually, I was scared of this bird, but at the same time I had an irresistible urge to see one, even catch one. Floyd and I would look for owls in hollow trees that had large "peckerwood" (woodpecker) holes in them. As you might know, owls are nocturnal. We did all our hunting in the daytime—fat chance we had of finding any and we never did. At nighttime, when they would make their eerie calls, it would scare us out of our "gourds". Screech owls made a quivering noise—it was positively the "scariest" sound ever! As I said, I never caught an owl—but one day one caught me.

There was an opening to the attic in one of our bedrooms. For whatever reason, I was attempting to climb up into the loft and had put my hand into the opening. Yeow! A barn owl, which had taken up residence there, promptly sank his claws into the back of my hand! If I had any wits they were quickly scared out of me. Did I say this was fun?

Fishing: What I liked best about fishing was eating what we caught. As a lad, I had to be the world's worst fisherman. I would get so excited when a fish began to nibble at the bait I would jerk the pole up so hard that invariably the hook would come out of the fish's mouth. I enjoyed it anyway.

Wagon Ride: Riding in our wagon was always a treat. It was especially nice when we crossed a fairly deep creek. Letting our feet drag through the water as we sat on the back of the wagon was "cool" man!

Playing in the Cotton: After the cotton was picked, it was stored in a large utility shed or barn. A huge bin was built inside the barn. The cotton was dumped into this bin up to a height of about seven feet. On rainy days, my brothers and I liked to play in this sea of cotton. We could dig all the way down to the barn floor. Tunnels were formed along the floor, then upward to the top of the cotton. Everything was just "peachy" until someone caved the openings in, leaving you trapped! Fearing we would suffocate, we would frantically begin to dig upward and out.

Playing in the Hay: We did a considerable amount of playing in the hay but it was never as pleasurable as digging in the cotton. Pieces of hay would get in your pants or shirt and be real scratchy. Once you became hot and sweaty, the fun was over.

Eating Watermelons: Each year Daddy would raise a large patch of watermelons. A number of varieties were planted. Our favorite was definitely the Stone Mountain. This melon grew to be quite large. It was a very dark green in color and had a bumpy skin. Growers rarely planted this exceptional melon for commercial purposes mostly because of its size and shape.

The Stone Mountain had the most wonderful flavor. My mouth got to watering just thinking about it. Daddy had several ways of determining when it was at its peak of ripeness. He would scratch the melons underbelly (a light colored spot), check the stem and then perform the ultimate test, "thump it". I use this time-tested method myself.

The watermelon was pulled the day before it was to be devoured. We would bring it to the house and place it in a cool spot. At times it was lowered down into our well.

The next day after our noon meal "Old Stoney" was placed on the picnic table out under the chinaberry tree. My brothers and I took our seats and watched the melon surgeon do his thing. Daddy would take his big butcher knife and stab it into the melon's end and bring it up and over the top. You could hear a popping sound as the Stone Mountain split apart. A rich sweet aroma wafted up into our nostrils, intensifying our mouth-watering anxiety.

Once the melon was halved, Daddy took the butcher knife and carved a huge hunk from the center of one of the halves and quickly disappeared. My dear Mama or an older brother cut the remaining melon into slices and the feast began. Burp!

Kite Flying: Our kites were homemade. Two thin sticks, a sheet or two of newspaper, some flour paste, a thin strip from an old sheet, and a large ball of string were all that was needed. Oh, yes, you would need a very strong wind to get these kites airborne. Once our creations were high in the sky, we were seldom able to bring them back in. It was always heartbreaking when the kite went down. Sometimes they would land in swampy areas and sometimes they just nestled in a tall pine tree and stayed there. All in all though, kite flying was a thrill. I well remember those days.

The Weed: A weed resembling a horse's tail grew along roadsides and fences in our area. We would sometimes use it as a broom. Over the years this unique weed has been the source of untold joy to thousands of young children. We cut the rather tall weed down and tied the ends of a two-foot string around the large end of it. Next we placed the weed between our legs, and as we held the loop in one hand .we slapped the rump of our horse and shouted, "Hi yo silver, away!"

With our God given imagination, we had transformed a rather useless weed into a great white horse. Amazing! As soon as little country boys and girls were old enough to walk and run, they would be seen riding that lowly dog fennel weed.

Gear on a stick: A small gear about six inches high, from an automobile engine, was stuck onto the end of a slender stick. Sitting cross-legged we would spin the stick around in an arc. The cogs on the gear would throw the dirt back, just as a car's wheels might. We would make little mounds of dirt for hills and puddles of water for creeks. We pretended we were driving a car. Let your imagination visualize what I have described. We had a great time with that stick and little wheel. You would have too if you lived back then.

~ *Happy Times* ~

Easter Egg Hunt: Offie Jones ran a little country store and gas station. One of his promotions was the yearly Easter egg hunt. Offie and his helpers hid both boiled eggs and candy all over his property. Some of the eggs were wrapped in gold colored foil. Should you find one of them, it could be redeemed for a prize. The egg hunt was for children only and did we have fun! Many times the candy eggs were covered with what Georgia is noted for, mean old feisty biting ants! Those creatures loved that candy as much as we did. We would just dust them off and enjoy our finds.

Corn Roasting: Fresh corn that was a little hard would be placed in the wood stove's oven and baked. It was necessary to rotate the ear to get a uniform brown color. The corn would be in the oven until it was almost burnt. Try it sometime. It's delicious "munching". South Georgia folk would call the corn "row-sen-neers," meaning "roasting ears". I love it!

Parched 'n Popped Corn: Cold wintry evenings were ideal times for parching or popping corn. An old fashioned popper was held over the coals in the fireplace and shaken. If field corn was used, there would soon be a pleasing aroma in the room. Indians and Civil War soldiers ate a lot of parched corn. Popcorn was always a great treat. Four hungry brothers consumed quantities of this goody!

Popcorn Balls: Mama would make big popcorn balls during the Christmas season. We would hang them on the tree as ornaments. On Christmas Day my brothers and I would receive the popcorn balls as gifts. My little sister shared in this treat as well.

Peanuts: You surely know that former President Jimmy Carter was a peanut farmer. Mr. Carter's farm was not very far from our own. I sometimes tell friends that the President and I went to different schools together.

Daddy was not a peanut farmer but he did plant large amounts of peanuts every year. I could hardly wait until they matured. We would eat them raw as soon as they were pulled from the ground. Boiling them while they were still fresh was another way of preparing the peanut. (To this day, I love them boiled as do most of our grandchildren, especially Tony!)

Most folk prefer to eat their peanuts roasted or parched. Just for the record, peanuts are not a nut but a legume, related to peas and beans. They grow on a thick cluster of small leaf vines. A beautiful yellow flower blossoms on a small stem. When the flower dies, it leaves behind a little bud. The stem then grows downward and burrows itself into the ground. A peanut will develop in the soft or loose soil. Peanut brittle is my absolute favorite way of eating peanuts!

Sugar Cane: We raised cane for making syrup, not sugar. Cane grew to a height of about eight feet. The usable portion was around six feet long. The stalk was divided into sections. A joint would separate each section, very much like bamboo. A hard outer layer protected the extremely juicy pulp inside. We peeled the outer layer off, cut the pulp up into small pieces and chewed it. Cane juice is ever so sweet and delicious. The pulp would be spit out after we had extracted every drop of juice.

Our Daddy would occasionally permit us to have some cane to chew but it was never enough to satisfy our desire for that sweet stuff. Not bad (but oh so clever) boys could surely find a way to get their fill of this nectar, and they did. My brothers would pull the soil away from the cane, cut a stalk down, and carefully put the dirt back. I hasten to point out that the cane stalks were not much more than an inch or two apart. The boys might cut down more than one stalk but always at a different spot. Need I tell you what would happen if they were caught? So, did I obtain cane in the manner just described?

No, not exactly. But should I happen on a scene of pilfering, my silence could be bought, if the price was right. Let's say, two or three sections?

Wild Grapes: Growing wild in southeastern United States is the Muscadine grape. Southerners have been making wine from this fruit for centuries. The vine may grow fifty or more feet up into a tall tree. The grapes have a dark maroon color and may also exhibit some red and purple. The leaves are small compared to other varieties.

We would tromp through the woods for hours looking for Muscadine's. The juice from these wild grapes was tasty, but a note of warning must be sounded for first time tasters—I say tasters, not eaters. Should you swallow the meaty inside of the Muscadine, dire consequence will result. You will develop the affliction most Civil War soldiers experienced—"the runs."

Plum Pig Out: In a corner of one of our fields and, beside the road was a large plum thicket. Both red and yellow wild plums grew there in abundance. As soon as this little fruit would ripen, my brothers and I could be found in the thicket. When the plums could not be picked from the ground, we climbed up into the little tree's branches. If you are the least bit squeamish, you might want to pass on partaking of these plums. Why? Because they well might contain a worm. Being experts at plum eating, a quick glance assured us that the plum was worm free. Besides, "what you don't know won't hurt you" or so they say. My brothers and I ate an awful lot of plums and never saw one worm.

Homemade Ice Cream: How easy it is nowadays to have ice cream. Just open the freezer and scoop some out of a carton. While dining out, ask your server for a dish of it. Believe me, it wasn't always that easy to obtain. Turning the ice cream freezer was hard work, very hard work! But the reward was "delicious"!

Syrup Makin': A great deal of work was involved in making syrup. Even though it was a demanding project, it was interesting and it was fun. In our syrup making building, Daddy had constructed a furnace with a large, built-in saucer-shaped metal dish. The dish's capacity numbered several gallons. Sugar cane juice was poured into the saucer and a fire was lit in the furnace. As the cane juice began to boil it would slowly thicken. Using a gallon dipper, Daddy would dip into the golden liquid, pouring the syrup back into the dish repeatedly. Once the syrup reached a certain viscosity, the fire was doused immediately. If you cooked the syrup too long it would turn to sugar. Some batches were ruined but most were not. It was a tedious and interesting process.

~ Buggy Sailing ~

My father kept a buggy in one of our barns, which I never saw hitched to anything. In all probability it was a relic from Daddy's past, which he kept because of nostalgia. Occasionally the buggy would be brought out, dusted off, and returned to its resting place in the barn. We would sit in it at times and imagine a beautiful shiny black horse was pulling us. Pretending was *lots* of fun.

It always seemed like such a shame and a waste to see that old buggy just parked there. How I longed to ride in it. My brothers, more than likely, felt the same way. Never did I think that one day we would all be riding down the road in Daddy's buggy. Our parents had gone away and left us to fend for ourselves. I'm sure we had been duly warned to stay out of trouble, and we very likely promised we would be good.

The day was very windy and clear—a good time for some-

thing, but what? On days like this you could see "whirlwinds" racing across the fields. It was fun to chase that spinning vortex. Jumping into the "whirlwind", you could feel the energy it was producing. It may have been after one of these experiences that a brilliant idea was conceived.

My brothers began rolling the buggy out onto the road. An old sheet was wrapped around the shafts and tied securely. As the forks were raised the buggy started moving immediately. Two of my brothers grasped the forks in order to steer the vehicle. We were all now in the buggy as it sped down the road. Faster and faster we sailed. The expression on our faces was one of amazement and pure joy. We had never in our lives experienced this kind of fun!

We looked at one another as if to say, *"Can you beat this?"*

After a lengthy ride, the wind slackened and the buggy came to a stop. Putting the shafts down, the buggy was pushed back to its starting point. I don't recall how many times we sailed down that road, but I'm sure it was several. As the old saying goes, "everything must come to an end". Another saying is "all's well that ends well". You can forget the latter. This story did not end well.

The final ride for the day began like all the others. Away went buggy and riders. At the end of this long stretch of road was a slight turn. On previous trips, it had been negotiated with relative ease. Approaching this bend, my brothers attempted to turn the buggy, but to no avail. *It went straight into the ditch.* There was the sound of things being broken. Fortunately for the riders, it was not their bones. Apart from bruises, we were all in one piece. The same could not be said for the old buggy. It was wrecked! We were in for it! The old wrecked buggy was dragged back to the barn. It would never intrigue us again. Our buggy-riding day was over.

"So what happened when your father came home?" you ask. Strange as it may seem, I have absolutely no idea. Remembering one trauma in a day's time is enough.

~ Other Pastimes ~

Fireflies: What youngster has not been amazed and delighted by this insect? My brothers and I would put dozens of them in a fruit jar. Did you call this beetle a lightning bug? So did we.

Looking for Guinea Eggs: Did you ever see a guinea hen? We had a large flock of these fowl on our farm. Guineas are very noisy and excitable. They make excellent "watch dogs". If someone approached the flock, they began making loud shrill sounds. Although the guineas are edible, we never ate them or their eggs. (I don't know why). So where does the fun come in? It was looking for their nests. Once we found a nest it would usually contain a dozen or more eggs. Mrs. Hen begins to cackle as soon as she lays an egg. *Not so the guinea hen*. To do so, she would give the nest's location away. A fox, weasel, dog or small boy would find the nest in a jiffy. After laying her egg, the clever guinea hen will travel quite some distance before beginning to cackle. There would be no need to look for the nest in the vicinity of her cackle.

Pig Pets: What could be cuter than a small pig? Actually, the title of this story is somewhat misleading. Daddy would not permit us to have a pet pig. He would have had a conniption if we brought a pig into the house

But sometimes we would pick the little piglets up and stroke them. You need have no fear of being bitten. They were absolutely harmless. When the pigs were a few months old, you could gently scratch their tummies and they would slowly roll over on their backs—almost like they were in a trance– maybe they just went to sleep.

Story Reading: I loved to read stories, but we had very few books, and there were no libraries around. We did have a six-volume set of encyclopedias, so I looked at the pictures in those even before I could read them.

Corn Husking: Sometimes we had a big "corn husking party" when many neighbors and their families were invited. All of our unshucked corn was dumped into a huge pile in front of our house. Chairs and benches were placed around the pile of corn. Tables were set up and loaded with goodies, such as cakes, cookies, candies and lemonade made with real lemons.

The party got underway about dusk. Lanterns were lit and a large bonfire was started. We children would begin playing games. Hide and seek and Tag were nighttime favorites. Folks took their seats around the corn pile. They were mostly men.

Scattered among that mound of corn were varicolored ears. We called this Indian corn. If in the process of shucking, you should find a colored ear, it could be redeemed for a prize. Prizes might be a jar of canned blackberries, pears, pickled peaches, etc. Two colored ears could be worth a pie. Unless there was an argument or a flare up of tempers, all would have a gay old time. We boys were very happy about the party. A lot of corn was husked and we wouldn't have to do it.

Flying Insects: Most of us have seen model airplanes. Some are flown by remote control and others fly some by long, hand held wires. Back in the early 1930's we had never heard of model planes, at least not in my "neck of the woods".

We did, however, fly something other than kites. *We flew insects.* Yes, I said insects, plain old bugs. Our favorites were June bugs and Cicadas. If these were scarce, horseflies would do in a pinch. With a spool of Mama's white thread in our pocket, we set out to catch our bug. The cicada, or locusts as we called them, were the most desirable because of their looks and size. Once our insect was in hand, the thread was tied around the bug's middle. Ten to fifteen feet was a good length for flying.

Holding one end of the string, we would toss our imaginary plane into the air. Around and around, up and down the bug would fly. It may have been a cruel thing to do but, quite honestly, we never gave that a thought. We were just having fun. The cicada was by far our best flyer.

~ *The Airplane* ~

My brothers and I were doing something around the house when we heard a strange noise. It sounded like an old truck way off in the distance. Considering where the racket was coming from, we knew it was something else. No roads were in that direction. The noise grew louder and louder. Whatever was coming our way was getting very close. We stood mystified and scared "to boot"! We anxiously waited to see what it was. *Suddenly an airplane appeared!* We knew about air-

planes but had only seen pictures of them. This was a slow flying biplane. You could see the goggled pilot with his scarf flapping wildly behind his head.

As soon as the aircraft appeared, we began jumping up and down and yelling at the top of our voice. We ran out into the field throwing dirt up into the air and shouting. It was all to no avail. The pilot most likely never saw us. We returned to the house somewhat disappointed but at the same time all keyed up with excitement. A real plane had flown over our farm. My brothers and I would be talking about this well into the night. It would be tomorrow's topic of conversation as well. Here I am, eighty and more years later, still talking about seeing my first plane.

After seeing that airplane, a longing to soar up into the clouds became my passion. Later in life I had the privilege of flying planes myself. It was a thrill!

"They that wait upon the Lord shall renew their strength;
they shall mount up with wings as eagles; they shall run
and not be weary; they shall walk and not faint".
- ISAIAH 40:31

Trips

~ Hazlehurst ~

Today, young boys and girls go on long trips with their parents. Some even visit other countries. During the early 1930's, poor farm families rarely went further than the County seat. Children grew up never having gone more than ten or twenty miles from their birthplace.

Hazlehurst, Georgia, is the County seat of Jeff Davis County and my birthplace. This was my favorite place to visit. I had two half brothers who lived just outside of the city. Both of these men ran small businesses—with bootlegging as a "side line". Carl, the younger one, was the most involved in the moonshine business and often got into trouble. His two sons, Julian, and Curtis and I had many fun-filled and exciting times playing together. Their father ran a gas station and garage along Highway 341. A large junkyard adjoined his garage.

Coleman, the older half brother, owned a gas station and small store, with a one chair Barber Shop attached. He and his wife Lera had three children, Ardith, Calvin and Jean. Calvin and I were about the same age. As young boys, we had formed a strong bond between us. Austere fathers may have been an element that drew us together. You be the judge.

~ Coleman's Fury ~

"Moon shiners" produced and sold illegal whiskey. The alcohol was made and sold covertly to avoid a high government-imposed tax. Corn whiskey may have been the most popular illegal "hooch". Making the "white lightning" was a way of life in some southern states. You don't have to be terribly bright to know why they made it at night. Hence—"moonshine".

During one of my visits with my nephew Calvin, my half brother Coleman's son, I opened the door to Coleman's barber-shop and peered inside. Looking around I spied two or three full gallon jugs. The contents of the vessels I did not discern nor did I seek to know. I was about to leave when Coleman screamed, "Get out– you---!" Believe me, I wasted no time in relocating.

Calvin was informed of his Daddy's rage. We agreed that he had "three sheets to the wind," that is, *he was drunk*. It was always a good idea to stay out of Coleman's way when he was drinking. In the afternoon, my nephews Julian and Curtis came to visit. Their home was not more than a mile away. The morning episode was largely forgotten as the four of us engaged in play. After supper about dusk, we were all playing around out by the highway. Coleman had not been seen since that early morning encounter and we were having fun.

Suddenly, he appeared from out of nowhere! It was obvious from his countenance that an ill wind was blowing. Ignoring the other boys, Coleman made straight for me. I stood frozen in my tracks. It must have been that my half brother threw me to the pavement, for I found myself being held by my ankles. In the next instant, Coleman was swinging me round and round. Every now and then my head would bounce off the road. Calvin was crying and pleading with his father to stop. To this day I can hear him saying, " Please Daddy, don't kill him, don't kill him!" Calvin was expressing my own senti-ments. The prospect of dying at the hands of a drunken half brother was horrifying.

As quickly as it started, my violent ordeal ended. Coleman dropped me to the ground and walked away. Apparently some degree of sanity had returned to his sick mind. Certainly God was observing this scene and ended it. How thankful I was.

> *"With the Lord there is mercy."*
> - PSALM 130:7

～ *A Political Rally* ～

In 1932, a huge political rally took place on the Jeff Davis County Courthouse grounds. The citizens of Hazlehurst were present in large numbers. Signs, colorful banners and bunting adorned the many booths. Flags were flying everywhere, especially the Confederate one.

A platform was filled with dignitaries and candidates. Speakers were busy extolling their accomplishments and virtues. It was indeed a gala occasion. I had never attended a political rally before, nor have I since. So why was I there? My parents, who lived in a different voting district, must have come just for the excitement. We probably spent the night with Carl or Coleman.

What made this event so attractive to me was the food—it was *"all free"*! Ice cold lemonade, fresh fried fish and if I am not mistaken, delicious southern style potato salad. The fish was fantastic. I began gorging myself with this delicacy. *Then it happened*! A large fishbone became wedged between my upper and lower teeth. I tried desperately to remove it, to no avail. The bone was solidly stuck!

It didn't take long for panic to set in. I began running wildly, crying and looking for my mother. Not being able to close my mouth, intelligible speech was almost impossible. As I called for Mama, it no doubt sounded like gibberish to those who heard my frantic cries. A few good Samaritans attempted to ascertain my problem, but it was Mama I wanted.

Mama loved me. She bound up my wounds and comforted me when I was frightened. No one in this whole wide world cared about me like Mama did. After considerable time Mama was found, and at last the bone was removed. Happily, activities resumed.

~ *Hidden Booze* ~

Rarely was a trip to Hazlehurst not enlightening. What my nephews didn't tell me about their father, I could readily observe for myself.

The Great Depression was a time of severe deprivation. Poor farmers struggled to provide basic needs for their families. In some instances, heads of households resorted to dishonest means. No father wanted to see his loved ones go hungry. My half brother Carl was no exception.

Carl was raised on a farm but never cared to pursue that kind of work. At an early age he would haul fruit and produce out of Florida and sell it on northern streets. As time went on, he purchased a filling station and garage—a quick way to lose your shirt, some would say. Carl's detractors underestimated his ability. "There's more than one way to skin a cat" may have been his motto.

The depression was in full bloom but surprisingly, the filling station and garage stayed in business. In fact, it appeared to prosper. Carl seemed to have that "money making" touch. Owning a business, home, car, truck, and smoking expensive cigars spoke loudly of his success. Not rich, mind you, but not hurting.

Not everyone was ignorant of my brother's good fortune. They knew where his money was coming from and it *wasn't* the filling station profits. Others could have done equally as well in their business if they were willing to take the risk! Carl was "bootlegging"!

He had a big auto junkyard. There was a sea of old jalopies from the garage to his home—a good fifty yards wide and maybe seventy yards deep. It was a perfect place for stashing "hooch". Many of the rusted heaps had no wheels and rested flat on the ground. The seats and floorboards of these cars were removed and a good-sized hole was dug. Jugs of whiskey were placed in the cavity. Seats and floorboards were then put back in place. Care was taken to make the scene look normal. Several cars might be used to hide the whiskey.

Federal agents would search Carl's property but never located his hiding places. Perhaps if rewards had been offered, a "rat fink" might have squealed.

~ Pelting Hobos ~

Behind Carl's garage was a deep cut for the Macon-Brunswick Railroad Line. Trains traversing this route would begin to slow down as they neared Hazlehurst's city limits. The cars were barely moving as they passed the cut or embankment. Hobos could be seen sitting in boxcar doorways and others lying in the open sand cars. Most of these men were not bums. They were traveling from place to place in search of jobs, as work was difficult to find. Not having the price of a fare, hopping a slow moving freight train would be their only means of getting around the country. My brother Kenneth was once jailed for "hopping a freight". The fine was five dollars. He was kept in jail until Mama sent him a "fin".

Julian and Curtis had it much easier than the Land brothers. They may have had too much idle time. Noting the hobos on the train, Julian decided to have some *"fun"* (?). He piled some small rocks on the bank overlooking the railroad. Curtis, being a follower, like myself, went along with this nefarious plan. When the train whistle sounded loudly, the boys hastened to their spot on the bank, and began pelting the riders down below. The hobos did not take this lightly! Jumping off the train they began throwing rocks at their tormentors. When things got hot for the two boys, they ran and hid in one of the old "junkers". The hobos, not wanting to lose their ride, returned to the train! These skirmishes were frequent, but thankfully, no one was ever seriously injured. This was not my idea of amusement!! But, "boys will be boys", they say.

Many ballads were written during the Great Depression. These poetic narratives often told the story of the poor man's struggle—his heartaches, disappointments and weariness. One song I liked to sing when I was a boy was about a hobo. I'm not quite sure of the words but it went something like this:

"All around the water tank
Waiting for a train.
A thousand miles away from home
Standing in the rain.
I walked up to a brakeman
And gave him a line of talk.
He says if you've got the money
I'll see that you don't walk.
I haven't got a nickel
Not a penny can I show
Get off, get off, you railroad bum
And he closed the boxcar door."

- BY JIMMY RODGERS

~ Dear Addie ~

The times I visited Julian and Curtis were made more enjoyable by the kindness of Addie, my half-brother Carl's wife. She would drive us to a large creek where we could frolic in the cool water. A picnic lunch, a soda pop and just maybe some ice cream might be served up. It was amazing to see Addie driving that big truck. The vehicle had a wooden cab with no doors. A large gas tank rested where you ordinarily see the dash. The truck had solid rubber tires. A chain from the engine to the axle turned the wheels. If that old "Federal Knight" exceeded twenty miles per hour, it would surprise me.

It was a pleasure to visit her in Hazlehurst—she enjoyed making us happy. At one point in Addie's life she became very ill. Her pain was so severe that morphine was the only thing that gave her relief. This dear lady suffered thus until the day of her death. She perished in a house fire some years later.

~ A Trip to Baxley ~

This "emerald city" was filled with music, excitement, colorful people and mystery. Who would not wish to visit this enchanted place? The town of Baxley had no yellow brick road. You would encounter no scarecrow, tinman or lion on its streets. But, for a young country boy, Baxley was a magical place. The sights, sounds and even its distinctive smell were exhilarating. One might say, intoxicating.

Nothing raised the level of excitement among us like being told "we're going to town." Our jubilant spirits soared high. Mama's declaration would be given two or three days in advance of the proposed trip. "You're not going if you don't do your chores!" Mama would say. This admonition was a clear case of parental behavior control. At least it helped to keep us in line for a time.

Country folk went to town infrequently but it was always on a "Satterday." This would be their day to strut. Some men dressed in their Sunday go-to-meeting clothes. Others wore their best overalls and brogans. The ladies were adorned with colorful bonnets and freshly washed print dresses. The "octagon fragrance" seemed to waft up from every passer-by.

The big day finally arrived. Up bright and early, we ate our breakfast quickly. The wagon was hitched up and we all piled in. Daddy slapped the mule's rump with the reins saying, "giddyap!" We were off to see the wizard of Baxley.

The town was approximately ten miles away and would take us about two hours. Our mule had one speed—slow. Once at the ford, Daddy would stop the wagon so our mule could refresh herself. It was inevitable that one of us would wind up in the stream too. Whether we slipped or were shoved mattered little to the wet one. He would dry out long before we reached our destination. The usual amount of quarreling, quibbling and fussing went on in our wagon. Two hours in such close quarters brought out the worst in us.

Daddy stayed on old dirt roads most of our journey. Eventually we came to U.S. Route Number One. This highway was paved and with a few autos buzzing along, thankfully, the old mule did not spook easily. Even with your eyes closed, one would know we had reached town. The chatter of sparrows was constant and loud. This little bird, most likely a chipping sparrow, was fond of inhabited areas. Having arrived at our "emerald city", we secured the mule at a designated hitching post. Since our stay would be lengthy, provisions for our mule were brought along. Mama had prepared victuals for our own consumption as well.

At this juncture, I'll begin relating some of my memorable

experiences in Baxley. They cover a four-year span but are not in sequence.

~ The "Human Fly" ~

He would scale tall buildings, using only his bare hands. Walking atop the facades was part of his breathtaking act. All this while blindfolded! No, it wasn't Superman. The Krypton kid was not yet on the scene. Billed as the "Human Fly", he would perform his daring feats right here in Baxley.

The city's storeowners had hired the "phenom" to attract would-be purchasers. Their promotion seemed to have worked by the looks of things. The sidewalks on Main Street were packed with locals and yokels. All had come to see the "human fly".

The performance was slated to begin around three in the afternoon. We waited and waited, and waited some more. When will he arrive seemed to be one of the questions upper-most in our minds. Will he come at all? I was thinking. "A watched pot never boils" Mama always said.

Finally, a big black car pulled up in front of the bank across the street. As all eyes focused on the vehicle, a man dressed in black got out of the car. *It's him! It's him*, the crowd exclaimed. The "human fly" began checking the buildings' masonry and seemed satisfied with what he saw. As I watched in awe with mouth open, the "fly" began his ascent. Up and up the wall he went. We were witnessing what we all had come to see. It was so spectacular you could scarcely believe your eyes! The citizens of Oz would have been impressed.

Reaching the top, the agile climber was greeted with loud applause. The star graciously bowed to his admiring audience. An assistant, who appeared on the roof, tied a blindfold over the "fly's" head. Standing on top of the facade's capstone, our star began to walk. With every teeter a chorus of "oohs" and "aahs" would ascend up. At the building's corner, fly man reversed himself and started back. More "oohs" and "aahs" were heard following each unsteady movement. Back at his starting point, the "human fly" waved to the appreciative onlookers. This concluded the entertainer's performance.

Some years ago I read a story about another "human fly". While climbing the side of a tall building, he reached up for what he thought was a brick but it was a " spider's web"!

That human fly lost his balance and fell to his death.

"On Christ the solid rock I stand
all other ground is sinking sand."
- HYMN BY EDWARD MOTE

— *Caroline Miller* —

Mama frequently spoke of an acquaintance of hers who lived in Baxley whose name was Caroline Miller. Caroline was an author who won the 1933-1934 Pulitzer Prize for her novel "Lamb in His Bosom". Carrie, as she was affectionately called, had three sons—William D., Nip and Tuck. She would put her children in the backseat of her car and drive around the countryside in search of food bargains. While among the rural folk, they would speak together of their various hardships and those of their parents. Carrie was a willing and sympathetic listener. After hearing of the struggles and courage Georgia's early pioneers exhibited, Carrie was moved to write about these dauntless people. She would sit in Barnes Drug Store on Saturdays interviewing many of the rural visitors. Much of the material for her novel came from such sources. There is little doubt in my mind as to how Caroline and Mother met. It is only reasonable to think she was one of those interviewed by the writer.

On one of our trips to Baxley, I distinctly remember crossing the railroad tracks and visiting in a nice lady's home. More than likely Mama had brought her some fresh vegetables.

Almost seventy years later I would again cross those tracks and go to what was once the home of Caroline Miller.

— 5 Cent Candy–Ice Cream & Boiled Peanuts —

Once in the fair city of Baxley, I would begin begging Mama for a nickel. No matter how impassioned my pleas were, they usually went unheeded, even when accompanied by a profusion of tears. So, what could you buy with one little buffalo?

A Babe Ruth Candy Bar: If you took *teenie weenie bites* you could nibble on this long time favorite for an hour. The temptation was to gobble the bar down quickly. Resisting this urge was a tremendous challenge. One I seldom won, I might add.

Ice Cream: Vendors sold their homemade ice cream on street corners. This was a terrific treat but you had to consume it quickly, lest it melt.

Boiled Peanuts: A real favorite of mine but we might have this delicacy at home, so I likely opted for one of the above. The peanuts were sold in a small brown bag with two little ears made by twisting the sack's corners together.

— Swan's Princess Theater —

A large banner hanging under the moving picture show's

marquee read, "twenty percent cooler inside." Placards and framed pictures announced coming events as well as what was presently being shown. Tom Mix, Buck Jones and a host of other cowboy stars could be seen galloping across the screen at the Princess Theater. There was that smell coming from within, a distinctive aroma that seemed to beckon you to come inside. How could anyone resist?

Oh, how I longed to see one of those thrilling westerns. The Princess, later called Roxy, was just across the street from the courthouse but it might as well have been in "Timbuktu". I was never to go inside. The admission price was more than Mama's budget would allow, I suppose. I would just have to be satisfied with the smell and the posters.

～ A Tobacco Auction ～

Daddy would bring our cured tobacco to the big warehouse in Baxley. Once there it would be put in large square baskets and tagged with our name. The baskets of tobacco were placed in long rows with that of the other sellers. Color was very important to buyers. A beautiful golden yellow tobacco would sell for much more. Extreme care had to be taken during the curing process.

When it was time to sell, the warehouseman, auctioneer and buyers would start down the aisle. Coming to the first basket, the auctioneer began to chant in what seemed to me, an unknown tongue. That unintelligible, staccato sounding voice was easily fathomable to the buyers. Each purchaser had his own unique way of bidding—a nod of the head, a tug of the ear lobe, finger movements, a wink or even a grunt. The auctioneer would spot the sign and continue until a sale was made. After the tobacco was sold, the warehouseman placed a card on the basket listing the buyer and the price per pound.

The farmers were anxious onlookers as the procession moved up and down the aisles. Many would groan when they saw at what price their tobacco sold. In 1932, twenty acres would gross about $1,800. A trip to the tobacco auction was always a thrill to me. I dare say it was not for the poor farmers!

Sad Times

~ The Little Blue Coffin ~

As we arrived at the house, which was scarcely more than a shack, caring friends and neighbors met us at the door. We were ushered into the small dimly lit parlor. Mama grasped the hands and spoke softly to the grieving young parents, offering our family's condolences. On a nearby table, clad in a long white nightgown, lay the still form of a tiny babe. She seemed to be asleep and so she was, *"asleep in Jesus"*. Though I didn't know it at that moment, this precious little soul was safe in heaven, secure and happy in the presence of her loving Savior.

Two shiny coins were placed over the baby's eyes. This would keep the eyelids closed. Light from a single kerosene lamp reflected off the bright coins, creating an eerie effect. This was my first occasion to see a lifeless human being. It was all so solemn and frightening. I never ever wanted to be around death again. I clung to Mama tenaciously and I wanted to go home. This, without doubt, had been the most disturbing night of my entire life.

The next day was Saturday and we were all going to town. This prospect raised our spirits immensely. The past night's fear, gloom and sadness, were rapidly fading from our thoughts. The family rose early and was anxiously awaiting their transportation. Finally a big stake truck, carrying a number of farm hands, stopped out in front of the house. Lickety-split my brothers and I climbed up and over the truck bed's side rails. Daddy, too proud to ride with his "younguns" and hired help, had reserved the front seat for himself and

Mama. No matter to us, we loved to stand behind the cab and feel the air as it struck our faces. It was fun to open my mouth and let the wind blow inside. At last Mama and Daddy took their seat. The driver, who would be paid for his services, looked back at his passengers as if to say, "Don't fall off!"

Putting the old truck in gear we sped off down the road.

Reaching the end of our property, the driver surprisingly turned onto a dinky road that led into the woods. As we bumped along we well might have been thinking there were others desirous of going into town. Before long we pulled up in front of the home our family had visited the past night. Silently we waited and wondered. A number of people came out of the house headed in our direction. One man was carrying a box covered with what looked like blue velvet. As the company reached the truck, a man climbed up to where we were and the box was handed to him. The young mother and father then joined the rest of us. Once more the truck started off and at last reached a highway.

As we rode along I could not keep my eyes from looking at what I knew was the "little blue coffin". Our hearts were sad and aching for we all knew who lay inside. The truck began to slow down and finally pulled off the road coming to a stop in an old cemetery. Just a few feet from us was a freshly dug grave. We could see all the way to the bottom from the truck's bed. Those who had joined us at the house climbed down from the truck. The blue coffin was passed to those standing below us. One of the men jumped into the rather shallow grave and was handed the little blue coffin. Placing it at his feet he climbed out of the cavity. A pile of green pine limbs lay nearby. These were tossed down into the burial place. This accomplished, the men, who had obtained shovels from some place, began filling the gravesite with dirt.

Beholding what had just transpired had a sobering effect on me. Somehow I knew I would never forget that "little blue coffin". Death was real and some day I would have to deal with it!

*"It is appointed unto men once to die,
but after this the judgment."*
-HEBREWS 9:27

*Jesus said: "Suffer little children to come unto me, and
forbid them not; For of such is the kingdom of God."*
- LUKE 18:16

～ *Polio–Numbered Steps* ～

Poliomyelitis (also called infantile paralysis) is an acute infectious disease, especially of children, caused by a viral inflammation of the gray matter of the spinal cord. It is accompanied by paralysis of various muscle groups that sometimes atrophy (waste away), and often causes permanent deformities and loss of function. Thankfully polio vaccine has now pretty much eradicated polio in the United States.

During my childhood, I spent more time with my brother Floyd than I did with any other person. This is understandable in light of our ages and circumstances. Born with an insatiable desire to investigate, he just had to check things out. Never mind that "curiosity killed the cat". Floyd's inquisitive mind kept him forever on the go and his number one disciple was right behind him.

One memorable day, Floyd and I set out in search of something interesting to do. We roamed the woods and fields for a considerable length of time but our exploration bore no fruit. To further add to our frustration, it was uncommonly hot, even in the wooded areas.

As the forenoon wore on, hunger had us heading for home.

Mama would have a delicious dinner ready at noon. Thankfully we arrived home in time for the meal. Otherwise Daddy *might* have made us go hungry. Punctuality at mealtime was an absolute with him.

After we ate, instead of relaxing a bit, off we went for more adventure. Floyd suggested we go to the ford and cool off. This sounded like great fun to me as we ran out of the house. Once at the ford, Floyd waded out to the middle of the stream and sat down. What was I to do but follow suit? Splashing and wallowing around in the cool water was so invigorating. Have you ever enjoyed this kind of fun? Believe me, it's the *"cat's meow"*. Having soaked ourselves through and through, we began *running* the mile back to our home.

Cecil greeted us as we came into the yard. He told us he thought there just might be an owl nesting in an old dead tree at the pond. Still panting from our most recent jaunt, Floyd and I sped off to see if we could catch one of those wise old birds. Surely that would be exciting!

The shallow pond was at the south end of our property. It was formed when several foot logs were placed end to end across a small stream. This site was near the headwaters of Bay Creek. The water flowed through dense forests on its way to the Altamaha River miles away. Numerous fishing holes and fords were located on the stream and its banks were thick with vines, bushes, trees and "cottonmouths".

Arriving at the pond, Floyd and I could see the old dead tree of which Cecil spoke. It was standing several feet out in the water. The top was broken off and no limbs remained on its weather-beaten exterior. About eight feet above the water's surface was a good-sized hole, an ideal spot for the owl family residence. But what were we to do? This question was answered almost immediately. Floyd jumped down into the pond and made for the tall stump. Climbing up to where the hole was located, without hesitation he thrust his hand inside the opening. Now I tell you plainly, I could not have done this. No way! Imagine what might have been in that hole. It could have housed a snake, bees, or even a scorpion. You definitely had to want an owl powerfully bad to do what my brother did. As Floyd removed his hand from the tree cavity, I could see that it was empty. Moreover, I didn't detect any sign of disappointment on his face.

For a third time, we started off for home. Though we would have nothing to show for all of our expended energy—nothing but a day full of memories, which sometimes can be priceless, don't you agree?

After a supper of corn bread and milk, Floyd and I began to play in the yard. My brothers had made a crude wagon with wheels of solid iron. How it came into our possession is a mystery to me. The sun was beginning to set and the air was noticeably cooler. Across from the well Mama's beautiful gardenia stood silently. Its large white flowers emitted a most wonderful sweet fragrance. God, who made flowers for Himself, surely was savoring this delightful aroma. The just and the unjust alike can all enjoy our great Creator's handiwork. As the long day drew to a close, I was tired, but there was very much to be thankful for.

As I stood near the gardenia plant, my brother playfully shoved the wagon directly at me. There was ample time and space for me to avoid being hit, but I didn't move. *I couldn't!* My mind was telling me to jump out of the way, *but my legs just didn't respond.* Mama, who had been watching us play, sensed that something was wrong. She wanted to know why I let the wagon hit me. All I could tell her was my legs wouldn't move. At that very moment, I think my dear Mama suspected what my problem was.

The following days I developed flu-like symptoms—fever,

headaches, vomiting, muscle aches and chronic diarrhea. By the time some of these ailments had subsided *I was no longer able to walk*. Mama arranged to have a neighbor, who owned a truck drive us to Baxley. Once there I was taken to the office of Dr. E.J. Overstreet. After listening to Mama tell about the various symptoms I had exhibited, the kind doctor examined me thoroughly, then he confirmed what Mama had secretly feared. I had *Infantile Paralysis!* The dreaded spinal Paralytic Poliomyelitis!

Within days I was completely paralyzed, unable to move even my head. Thankfully, I could open my eyes and mouth (never a problem there) and swallow. Arrangements were made for my treatment, which began immediately. A nurse came twice daily to bathe me with rubbing alcohol and massage my limbs, neck and trunk. Each morning a large bowl of oatmeal saturated with cod liver oil was forced down my gullet. Oh how I hated that concoction. Eventually a baby bed was obtained and I was placed in it.

The one thing I dreaded most during this lengthy ordeal occurred daily. After my morning treatment, I was placed in the baby bed and rolled into the parlor to stay while all the family would leave to work in the fields. Left all alone and helpless, a mortal fear would come over me. As I lay there straining to hear, the old house would begin creaking. With each creak, I imagined a "haint" was coming to get me or maybe it was the devil and he would cast me into hell. *I tried to scream, to cry out for help, but no sound would usher from my lips. "Mama, Mama please come and save me!" Every day it was the same. Every day I would lie there wishing I could tell someone about my fears.* Had I been able to communicate how frightened I was, maybe some would have laughed. My father and brothers had instilled in me the notion of "haints". Putting sheets over themselves and creeping into my room at night—I would be scared out of my wits. To my tormentors, it was fun. To me, it was unspeakable torture!

How grateful we all were that after a long period of time my speech slowly began to return. Also, I *gradually* regained some strength in my arms. Eventually I was placed on the floor and developed a rather unorthodox method of crawling.

～ *Coleman's Kindness* ～

One day my half brother and his family came to visit us. He had fashioned a pair of crutches out of pine limbs. Coleman stood me up beside the porch and put the crutches under my arms. While holding on to me, he encouraged me to attempt to walk. After numerous tries some progress was eventually made. Finally, I could walk with the crutches, unassisted! What a glorious day that was!

Coleman seemed to take a special interest in me and came again for another visit. I was in the front yard leaning against the porch. Coleman came over and took my crutches. "Now," he said, *"I want you to walk*!" Even though I wanted to desperately, it was impossible, *or so I thought*. Standing several feet in front of me, he began to coax me to take a step. *"Just one step,"* he said. After much urging and pleading, I put one foot forward. "Let go of the porch," Coleman exhorted me. Slowly and reluctantly, I removed my hands from the porch. Though fearful and unsteady, I took that first big step, then another and another. *At last I had walked once again!*

How unbelievably happy those few steps had made me feel. My cup was running over. All who were present shared in this joy and exuberance. God, who numbers our steps, was giving me additional ones. Coleman, who once sought to do me harm, had now shown me kindness.

"...Thy mercy is great above the heavens."
- PSALM 108:4

"...it is not in man that walks to direct his steps." Jeremiah 10:23
"A man's heart devises his way; but the Lord directs his steps.
- PROVERBS 16

— *The Face in the Clouds* —

Many young children acquire numerous fears. Some of them may be logical while others are illogical. Be they real or imagined, these bugaboos often have a devastating effect on a youngster's life. I had legions of childhood fears, and to make matters worse, a couple of phobias were added to the mix. Among living things, what frightened me most were snakes! Poisonous or not, these creatures terrified and petrified me.

Then there were the lizards! I once read that there are two thousand and five hundred species throughout the world. As little orphan Annie would say, "Leaping lizards!" The United States is host to ninety species. I'm convinced most of these critters were found between our house and the mailbox. Both skinks and swifts gave me the "willies". On my way to get the mail, I would spot blue skinks clinging to the sides of pine trees. Some blue skinks have bright red heads. At the sight of this reptile, I would take off running "lickety split". If that thing bit me, I would surely die, or so I reasoned.

Scorpions were another threat to my existence and this critter was found in abundance throughout our area. It was highly unlikely I would perish from a scorpion's sting, but you would have had a problem convincing me.

The very mention of wildcats and black panthers would cause my hair to stand on end. I think a face-to-face encounter with one of these fearful animals would have given me a heart attack. Thankfully, my path and that of the Black Panther never crossed. This beautiful beast was relentlessly hunted. Today it can be found in the Okefenokee swamp.

One day our dogs, Mutt and Jeff, and those of one of our neighbor's, had chased a wildcat back under an overhanging bank of a small stream. It was impossible for the hounds to get at the cat from its rear. A frontal attack was their only option. Each dog had attempted to go under the bank and straight at the bobcat. Each came back out yelping and with a very bloody snout. The barking and yelping dogs and the screeching, screaming wildcat created a very loud frenzy. The commotion did not fall on deaf ears. Soon my brothers, a couple of neighbor boys and I were on the scene. For obvious reasons, we remained observers. *That was one ferocious wildcat!* To involve one's self in this standoff might get your eyes scratched out. The better part of valor would be just to retire, which we did, along with the canines. Score one for the game and heroic bobcat.

Screech owls may be cute, fuzzy little fellows but the spooky, scary, quivering noise they make can frighten the pants off you, not literally of course. The sounds of a screech owl still give me "goosebumps".

Often in the summer, we would sit on our porch in the evening, listening to night sounds. You could hear katydids, crickets, owls, nighthawks, mocking birds, and an occasional wildcat. Off in the distance a whip-poor-will, the chuck-will's-widow or possibly an eerie screech owl could be heard. Scary stories would also be part of the evening's fare. The darkness seemed to induce as much fear as the storyteller. Sitting there on the old porch might be peaceful, exciting, enjoyable, and it was—but not always. So, what could turn a perfectly delightful evening into one of terror? It began like this. Everything was so serene, *so quiet*. Suddenly someone shouted, *"Look! Look down by the swamp!* See it?" All eyes immediately focused on the area being pointed out. What we all saw sent shivers up and down our spines. At least, that was decidedly my reaction. Most of us were scared out of our wits! A bright light, very much like that given off by a large lantern, came up out of the marsh. It began to bounce along the edge of the swamp. At times the light would rise several feet into the air. We were witnessing a phenomenon and it was ever so frightful! None of us knew what we were seeing, but we were certain we never ever wanted to see it again. Some would tell us it was a spook, others said it was a jack-o-lantern. Yet another called it a will-o-the-wisp. Superstitious country folks would not believe in any scientific explanation of the phenomenon, no matter how plausible. Scientists call the light an "ignis fatuus". They further say it appears at night over marshy grounds and is supposed to be caused by the combustion of marsh gas (methane). Now why do they say it is *"supposed to be"*?

Two phobias troubled me early in my life. One was the fear of water and the other the fear of night, also called Nyctophobia.

There was another fear that had a profound effect on my life in a positive way. I hated it with a passion because it vexed my soul, tormented my mind and instilled fear into me. As far back as my memory goes, I would have this recurring dream. The nightmare, and it was just that, would regularly trouble me until we moved away from the old homestead. At that time, I was nine years old.

On the Eastern side of our farm, there was a sandy road that went by our home. In my dream, as I would begin to walk toward our house, it would suddenly become dark, very much like it does before a rainstorm. When the darkness came, I would start to run but my feet seemed to slip in the deep sand.

I tried to run as fast as possible, but could make no headway. I desperately wanted to get home and to Mama. *"Mama, oh dear Mama! Please help me!"* Try as I might, no progress was being made. My cries to my mother would go completely unanswered. I was so afraid. As I struggled, I could sense that someone or some thing was behind me. Summoning up my last ounce of courage, I looked back to see what was there. What I saw was a gigantic "face in the clouds". It was terrifying! Suddenly hands from out of nowhere grabbed me up into the air and then cast me down into what seemed like a bottomless pit. Down and down I went, fully expecting to land in the flames of an everlasting Hell! This, however, would never happen. In every dream I would awaken at this point. At such a young age I knew beyond a shadow of a doubt there was a hell to shun. It would not be Mama who would come to my rescue. Even she was powerless to save me.

I did not know God or His Son, but I did know I was a sinner. I was a stranger to the Father of mercies, unacquainted with the God of love, the God of hope and the God of all grace. They would all manifest themselves to me in due time. *Hallelujah!*

The God of all grace gives me what I don't deserve.
The Father of mercies does not give me what I do deserve.

More Stories

~ The Migrant Sharecroppers ~

In the 1930's, sharecroppers were often migrant farmers who grew crops on rented land for a share of the profits. This usually amounted to about one half to three quarters of the net sales. The migrant and his family would supply the labor; the landlord would provide the land, a dwelling, farm animals, equipment, seed, plants, fertilizer and cash or credit for living expenses. Most often, garden plots were available. After the crops were harvested and sold, the farmer would repay the landlord for money advanced to him. Once the settlement occurred, the migrant would move to another area seeking work. As a result, another sharecropper would have to be found for the next season.

A couple hundred yards beyond our place stood a small weather beaten old shanty. Void of paint and with a rusty tin roof, this unimpressive dwelling would be "home" for our next migrant sharecropper. Many such structures as I have described can still be seen throughout the Deep South.

My brothers and I were told the day the farm family was due to appear. As soon as the sound of a motor vehicle was heard, we dashed off to the shanty. A sputtering, squeaking old truck came to a stop in front of the gate. As it did, steam began to spew from the radiator. It almost seemed to be giving a sigh of relief.

What a sight to behold. Everything the poor migrant farmer owned was piled high up on that dilapidated looking truck. Chairs, beds, boxes, washtubs, a crate full of chickens and many other household items were tied to the vehicle. A passel

of younguns, stuffed in among the dry goods, peeked out at us. Their eyes were open ever so wide, reflecting the curiosity pervading their minds. As children, we were all anxious to become acquainted. I was hoping at least one of our new neighbors would be my age—preferably a boy. Older kids would treat me as if I had the plague. And so they would come, all sizes, ages, looks and personalities. Some of the sharecropper folk would be friendly and fun to be around. Others might not be what you had hoped for. As in life, we must deal with the good and the bad.

~ The Painted Lady ~

In all of my six years I had never beheld anyone quite so lovely as the Sharecropper's wife. She was fabulously beautiful, and very fascinating. Upon first seeing her, I might well have exclaimed, "She shore is purty."

Her ladyship undoubtedly considered laboring in the fields to be beneath her dignity—at least she was rarely seen toiling in them. If the dear lady did make an appearance in the hot sun, a large bonnet would almost obscure her face. One so fair and delicate must not be exposed to the harsh elements—my mother and other female workers were.

The better part of our subject's time was spent indoors and you could usually find her sitting in front of a princess dresser, primping. What's more, I could be found nearby observing. The beautifying process would begin with the long tresses. Using a hot curling iron, her loveliness would patiently and skillfully make tightly wound ringlets. The curls hung down below her shoulders. Once the hair was done, she would focus on her lips. Removing the applicator from a Mercurochrome bottle, the fair lady would carefully and painstakingly begin painting her lips. There was no money for lipstick, so this reddish antiseptic served as a substitute and would last for a number of days. The final beauty treatment was an application of powder and rouge. The results of this charmer's artistry were fantastic! It well might have caused Venus to become jealous had she witnessed it.

Exciting and pleasurable as it was to see this exotic woman perform her magic, "there was a fly in the ointment". She had a four-year-old daughter who was at every performance. This child annoyed me to no end! She was forever saying, "One day I will be as old as you." I may not have been very bright but I was certain she would never be, and I kept telling this

nuisance it wasn't going to happen. It was all so exasperating. *"Some day I'll be as old as you,"* she taunted.

~ The Stand Off ~

It was well into the growing season and the crops were doing very fine, but there was friction between Daddy and the sharecropper. A dispute had arisen over some matter. It was probably just a difference of opinion that reasonable men

126

might have settled, but Daddy was not known to be a reasonable man. He didn't like to compromise or admit he was wrong. (I do believe the Land boys inherited an abundance of Daddy's stubborn genes). We were all working in the field, chopping cotton when "a bone of contention" flared up into a violent argument between the adversaries. Finally Daddy, who often tried to bluff his opponents, threatened the sharecropper with bodily injury via his shotgun. He menacingly remarked, "I'll blow your (censored) head off!" To Daddy's surprise, his antagonist responded, "I'll blow YOUR head off." Both men immediately fled to their respective houses, supposedly to arm themselves. Needless to say, my brothers and I were trying to decide which way to run. If there was going to be a shooting, we did not want to be the victims!

Mama left for the house to talk some sense into Daddy. This would not be a difficult task. By now our father realized what a terrible predicament he had gotten himself into. The sharecropper's wife would also calm her irrational husband down. There would be no "Hatfield and McCoy" shootout this day. I'm pretty sure my brothers were relieved.

Within a day or two after the big blowup, an old truck pulled up to the shanty. The farmer began loading his possessions onto the vehicle. As soon as the job was completed, the beautiful painted lady came out of the house carrying her four year old. She took her seat beside the driver and her husband got in the cab beside his wife. Slowly the creaking old truck started off down the road. The princess dresser could be seen secured to the vehicle's bed. There were no well wishes or goodbyes. I felt very sad as I watched the truck and its occupants disappear from view. I would never see the painted lady again and I would never see that little girl again. I would never hear her say, "Some day I'll be as old as you." I was right, she never would.

~ Short Lived Fortune (Freeman) ~

The only name I ever knew him by was Freeman. He came to help us with our crops and Daddy provided him with room and board. Even though Freeman ate his meals with us and occupied one of our bedrooms, he rarely spoke. I have absolutely no memory of anything he may have uttered. Now that is not to say we did not have an acute awareness of his presence. *We did.*

Freeman did his work around the farm and pretty much kept to himself, but this quiet man had a way of looking at you that gave us an uneasy feeling – something just short of fear. It wasn't long until we became extremely fearful of him and the sooner he left our home the better.

While he was performing his duties to Daddy's satisfaction, a severe problem was about to manifest itself. Freeman, who had gone some place on his day off, returned in the evening drunk as a "hoot" or, as we also say, "Soused to the gills." Staggering across the yard, Freeman collapsed on the porch and remained there until morning.

One day while I was playing under our front porch I spotted quite a number of coins scattered about. Almost instantly something told me how the money came to be there, and who the owner was. My conscience told me to return the money to whom it belonged. "He who hesitates is lost" goes the old saying. Greed over-powered me. I had found the money and it was mine! *All mine!* Looking furtively about, I began putting the coins into my pocket. Finding an empty snuff can, the loot was transferred into it. My next move was to find a good hiding place. Crawling back under our house to about the midway point, I placed my fortune on a supporting block and crawled back out.

Thinking about the situation, I began to wonder how I would be able to spend the money without being caught? How much money did I actually have? Could I trust anyone? I realized I had no answers. If others were informed of my good fortune, they would simply take it from me. What to do? At last, I devised a plan. I needed to know how much money I really had. I'd ask my brother Cecil a few questions, hoping he wouldn't become suspicious. My first question to him was, "If you had two quarters and two dimes how much would that be?" His response was seventy cents. Since I could not add very well, it was important that Cecil help me as much as possible. After all, I was only six years old. When he was not looking I crawled back under the house and took out two dimes. Locating my brother, I asked him "how much was two dimes and seventy cents?" Again he obliged me, and I returned to my hiding place for the third time. In the meantime, dear brother Cecil's curiosity had been sufficiently aroused. He stealthily followed me back under the house. As I turned to crawl back out, I came face to face with my brother! As they say, the "jig was up". "Give me all the money or I will tell Freeman and he will kill you." There would be no bargaining and no pleading. The little fortune was handed over with guilty, reluctant anguish and there was nothing I could do about it. After all, I didn't want Freeman to kill me.

"Let him that stole steal no more."
- EPHESIANS 4:28

~ To the Mailbox ~

I was often called upon to make trips to our mailbox, a little over one mile away. Being the youngest of four brothers and lazy to boot, my piddling work around the farm would scarcely be missed. So, the dreaded trek for the mail frequently became my allotted portion. Obviously my Mama and Daddy thought no harm would befall me. Quite frankly, I did not share their opinions concerning my welfare. Everything imaginable might well happen to me, none of which would be good. Simply put, I was afraid. My cruel and mandatory trips to the mailbox began when I was five or six years old.

Most of the time I walked but on rare occasions a mule was available to ride. The latter mode of transportation was definitely preferable. Actually, riding the mule could be enjoyable, barring the unforeseen. Arriving at the box, an attempt would be made to remove the mail without dismounting. The trick was to maneuver your beast into a position whereby you could lean over and extract the mail without falling. Mind you, this was no easy task. If you leaned too far, you very well might land on your head in the dirt below. Many such attempts were unsuccessful, creating another problem, how to get back astride the mule. A sycamore tree near the mailbox usually was the answer. Taking hold of the bridle, I would lead the mule over to a large overhanging branch of the sycamore, climb up the tree, shinny out on the limb to a spot directly above her back and drop down onto it. You might say I had it "made in the shade". A bridle has blinders, which prevents the mule from having side or rear vision. As soon as I would plop onto her back, it would frighten the mule and she would take off running back to our barn. Very often I wasn't able to hang on and would again wind up in the dirt.

It wasn't just the sight of a snake that scared me as I walked to our mailbox, there were numerous impressions left in the loose sand where the reptiles crossed the road. As soon as these markings were spotted, I would freeze in my tracks. If within earshot of the house, I would begin shouting for help.

More often than not, no one came to rescue me. If anyone did respond to my cries, they would stand afar off and tease me. There really was nothing to fear from those impressions, but I could not be convinced of that. As far as I was concerned, those horrible creatures were lurking nearby to strike me dead. One probable cause for my fear of snakes was my brothers who took great delight in throwing both dead and live ones at me. Thankfully, they were not the poisonous kind.

In spite of all the negatives associated with my perilous trips to the mailbox, some had a positive side. Even though I was unable to read initially, just opening the box and finding a package inside was like Christmas time all over again. It was so very exciting. My Aunt Ethel frequently sent us packages. Then there were the letters and every so often that famous, fabulous Sears and Roebuck catalog—a country boy's dream book. When the new edition arrived, the old one was destined for the outhouse.

In some ways a trip to the mailbox was a learning experience. Early on, the importance of knowing how to read was brought home to my psyche. One day I opened the mailbox and found a small package inside. Curious as to what it might contain, I began to pull at one end and to my surprise it came open. Inside were two long, flat bars of chocolate candy, each were divided into four sections. All at once I felt an irresistible urge to sample one of those bars. I bit into one of the sections. It was simply delicious. Before long I took another bite. At this point I realized I must consume the whole bar lest Mama or Daddy discover what I had done. The remaining bar was placed back into the box and the end resealed. I was hoping my thievery would go undetected. When I arrived back home Mama took the little package and began reading the information printed on it. E-X-L-A-X! "Did you eat any of this," she inquired. Noticing that she was not irate and even seemed to be smiling, I confessed to have eaten one bar. Upon hearing this, she burst out laughing and soon informed other family members. They too found my candy eating amusing, even downright hilarious. Well as you might expect, it wasn't long before my stomach began to rumble and I took off for the outhouse! My stay there would be quite lengthy but the Sears and Roebuck catalog was available and I could always look at the pictures. One day I hoped to be able to read and I would be aware of what E-X-L-A-X could do to a person.

~ The Watermelon Patch ~

A gloriously beautiful sunrise or a breathtaking sunset has always been a thrilling sight to me. Even as a small child. I could appreciate these phenomenal events. The sun's rays would sparkle on the dew of the longleaf pines as their source began it's trek across the sky. Dawn's radiant energy was like a new birth as it ushered in the beginning of another special day—a day of hope when dreams would be fulfilled. Everything seemed to be fresh, clean and invigorating. Then there was the sunset. The toil of the day had pretty much ended. The clouds became illuminated as the sun sunk deeper in the western sky—it was time to rest.

There was another magnificent sight that left me so awe struck I got goose bumps. Of all the things on our farm, there was nothing more delightful to behold than our watermelon patch. It was like a sea of monochrome green before our eyes. Many light and dark melons could be seen popping up among the vine's large leaves. Viewing and eating those delicious melons gave me immense pleasure.

In order to have a good crop of watermelons for the next year, the largest specimen would be singled out and given spe-

cial attention. Daddy placed straw underneath the melon to insure against rot, and on top to prevent sunburn. The watermelon was frequently thumped to ascertain its peak of ripeness. If pulled too soon, the seeds would be immature. We were all anxiously awaiting the day Daddy would proclaim the melon was ready to eat. Being sure to save every seed, it would be devoured with gusto.

A very young black lad would frequently come to our farm to perform certain chores. He was dependable and extremely bright, and his demeanor and work habits pleased my father immensely. Those who did such odd jobs could hardly expect more than fifty cents for their labors. At times, wages were augmented with a slab of sowbelly if it could be spared.

One day, after the young man completed his assigned tasks, Daddy paid him and suggested that on his way home he take a melon as additional compensation. The young worker kindly thanked Daddy and began his journey some two miles away. The trip was down a path that went by our watermelons. Arriving at the patch, he wasted no time in deciding which melon to take. *Carrying a round, sixty-pound watermelon two miles would be no easy task.* Sharing this humongous, delicious fruit with family may have been all the motivation he needed. Daddy soon discovered the loss of his prized seed-melon. My guess is he became irate, extremely so. Then again, maybe he just waxed philosophical but "don't bet the farm on it".

Many years later we had the opportunity to revisit this area. As we drove up to the modest little white house, I could hardly wait to speak with one of its occupants. His name was Wilbur Williams. We had met him earlier at the Mizpah Baptist Church. Barbara Williams and Willa Mae Harris told me Mr. Williams might have answers to many of my questions. I was looking for someone who had lived reasonably close to our home during the late twenties and early thirties. After being introduced to Mr. Williams, I asked him if my brother Floyd and I and our wives might call on him later that Sunday afternoon. He graciously consented, knowing full well what the purpose of our visit was.

Mr. Williams, whom I shall hereafter address as Wilbur, received us most cordially as we exchanged civilities. My sister Faye Blair, Floyd and his wife Ruth, Wilbur and his beloved wife, my wife Ruth and yours truly were present. As we sat there on the porch, I was anxious to begin the inquiries. Floyd attempted to record this important discussion, but unfortunately his equipment malfunctioned.

If I'm not mistaken, my first question to Wilbur was "Did you know my father?" This query opened a floodgate. Wilbur said that he did, and began to name every member of our family, including a half sister and her brother. This amazing man went on to give us a brief history of the Lands. We were flabbergasted! How was it this man could know so much about us? Seventy-five years had gone by since he had seen or spoken to any of us.

It is very unlikely that any family member shared with Wilbur any of the information of which he spoke. He had just overheard conversations and they became a part of his memory. We left Wilbur's home bewildered but happy. This dear, black brother had provided us with a touch of our past and we were grateful.

So where did Wilbur live in relation to our farm? His home was about two miles away. To get there, one would traverse some of our fields, make their way through a stretch of woods, cross a creek and begin a long rise to Wilbur's place. The journey would start by heading down a well-worn path that went by our watermelon patch!

Shortly after our visit, our dear brother Wilbur went Home to be with the Lord. His beloved wife was soon to follow.

~ He Died with His Spurs On ~

Scarcely a day passed that he could not be seen strutting amongst his seemingly devoted followers. Clothed in a beautiful and colorful coat that glistened in the bright sunlight, this fellow was impressive looking! There was an air of regality about his being. Two long razor sharp spurs jutted out from his skinny yellow legs. These formidable weapons seemed more than adequate to rout any would be challenger to his reign and realm. Thus adorned and equipped, one might say that his majesty was, *"The Cock of the Walk"*.

Unknown to this illustrious chicken house character, mortal danger was rapidly approaching. For Casanova and his little band of admirers, this would not prove to be Romeo's finest hour. Our feathery friend had seen his best days.

Returning home from school and armed with his trusty old slingshot, my brother, Floyd, was nearing the sharecropper's house. There, out by the well, the old rooster and company leisurely foraged. From a previous story you know the Land boys were not permitted to have slingshots. Floyd hid his before reaching home, some 200 yards away. He would need to act quickly.

Slingshot in hand, this sibling was determined to shoot something, anything that moved. There was no rationale for the senseless act that was about to occur. However, in my own assessment of the situation, Floyd's actions were predictable and as inevitable as the rising sun. A young boy and a loaded slingshot is a formula for disaster. Believe me, *I know*.

As Floyd passed the sharecropper's shanty he saw the chickens out by the well. The hens were busily scratching in the sand and weeds, hoping to find a tasty morsel. The ladies paid little heed to my brother. Their guardian, however, upon hearing the slightest sound or seeing any movement, stood up ever so erect. He cocked his head and began to look around. At that very moment, Floyd pulled the rubber bands back and let the stone missile fly. The rock struck the old red rooster squarely on his head, killing him instantly. In less time than it took for the projectile to reach its target, my brother was smitten with regret and remorse. He also knew what the consequences would be when Daddy learned of his despicable deed.

Shortly after Floyd arrived home, an irate sharecropper appeared at our door. He was ranting about the dead rooster. He contended vehemently and with no little measure of foot

stomping that Floyd had dispatched his bird! "He knew" because the killing occurred about the time Floyd was passing by. There was no need for such vehement accusation by the sharecropper – the Land boys were always guilty until proven innocent. Daddy would be easily persuaded of Floyd's guilt. I did not witness the punishment but you may be assured, it was most severe. My brothers and I were frequent visitors to the proverbial "woodshed" and could testify as to the agony experienced therein.

Floyd recently reminded me of the "old red rooster tale". It seems he has forgotten one amusing detail. The rooster was tossed into the farmer's well, *adding insult to injury,* so to speak. When I told him of my recollections, he allowed "that was a distinct possibility". One might readily conclude that the rooster jumped up onto the well's sideboards to crow and fell in. Now that sounds like a reasonable assumption to me. Daddy, always wary of his sons' account of events, was not buying. He chose to side with the distressed sharecropper.

"The Lord has said: 'Be sure your sins will find you out'."
- NUMBERS 32:23

~ *The Clay Eaters* ~

Believe it or not, there are folks who chew and eat moist fatty—textured clay known as Kaolin. This strange practice is common in many places throughout the whole world. It was prevalent among the very poor in Georgia and the Carolinas—and many still consume quantities of this "dirt". The clay can be purchased in some stores.

Debunked by the medical profession, clay eaters generally maintain that the soil contains curative properties. Even with the advancement of modern medicine, old cultural traditions refuse to die. Today's proponents might say, "If it was good enough for my Grand pappy, it was good enough for me".

At the end of our property, there was a long, sloping hill. Near the middle of the rise, the sandy topsoil had washed away, exposing a bank of reddish looking clay. There were streaks of dark blue and white running throughout the bank. Many times I would pass by this area and observe a black person busily digging into the clay and putting it into his mouth. Out of curiosity, I decided to sample some of the stuff. Surprisingly, it had little or no taste. Now, if I had only thought to bring along some sugar, who knows, we might have had a hillside of dessert on our place.

Clay is made up of many things. Hydrous aluminum silicate is one part of its composition. This kind of soil is essential for plant growth. My guess is that clay eaters often received positive results from that good old Georgia dirt. Hey! If you ain't tried it, don't knock it!

～ He Was Tetched ～

He was very old and stooped. His bent frame was likely a result of many years of honest toil. A thick, kinky "salt-n-pepper" beard, streaked with stains, covered much of his wrinkled face. The old man's clothing was soiled and tattered. Even in the mid summer heat, he wore a rumpled black coat and a well-worn straw hat pulled down around his black eyes, which further added to his mysterious appearance. If he had a wife or children, I was not aware of it. It may be that the old gentleman could not even speak. We had passed one another on the road various times but never exchanged words. Fear and timidity would be my excuse for not speaking. He chose not to acknowledge my presence.

"Tetched" as he was called, would emerge from his little shanty home and begin slowly ambling down the dirt road that ran by his house. He kept his eyes glued to the ground in front of him as he made his way along. Spying a colorful pebble at his feet, he would pick the stone up and put it into his pocket. To most of the locals, this would be strange behavior. I suppose it was because of this peculiar habit that the old man was called "Tetched." Could it not be that this dear soul saw in his stones something that all too many of us never see—*the beauty of our God's handiwork*? We would do well to ask ourselves just who is "tetched".

~ *The Search for Floyd* ~

Night had fallen and Floyd had not come home. Having missed his supper, dear Mama was becoming very anxious. The coal oil lamp in our parlor did very little to dispel the darkness or allay our fears. Needless to say, our spirits were troubled as we thought, *"Where is that wandering child?"* It was almost bedtime and I became painfully aware of how lonely and afraid I would be through the night without my brother, my protector and my friend beside me.

As I lay quietly on my bed, far off in the distance I could hear the haunting repetitive sound of a whip-poor-will. This mysterious, seldom seen bird with its distinctive call always frightened me. "Please come home brother Floyd," I well might have cried. Whip-poor-will, whip-poor-will, whip-poor-will and so it went into the night. Sleep at last overtook me, bringing relief to my troubled mind and weary body.

Morning came but no joy accompanied it—no joy to cheer our aching hearts. Dear Floyd was still missing. Daddy had searched the woods and looked into the many sheds and barns on the farm. Inquiries were made of our distant neighbors but this bore no fruit.

At last Daddy did something none of us ever thought he would do. Though he despised Offie Jones, he went to Offie's store and gas station, several miles away to inquire if he had seen anything of Floyd. Jealousy was the cause of my father's contempt. If my mother even looked at another man, Daddy's vile, jealous nature would flare up. In Mr. Jones' case, Mama was constantly being accused of having more than a passing interest in Offie. This was very debatable.

Down a little slope near our house was the tobacco barn and just beyond the barn, a huge cistern had been excavated. The water reservoir was eight to ten feet square and extremely deep, with its walls lined with logs. Planks covered the opening. If a person fell into this watery pit, he'd probably be unable to get out without assistance—it would be well nigh impossible to scale those slippery walls. We boys were absolutely forbidden to go near that dangerous place.

On the second or third day after Floyd's disappearance, Daddy decided to check out the cistern. Taking a long rope and a large three pronged grappling hook, I was asked to accompany him to the well site. After removing the covering, he fastened one end of the rope to the hook and dropped it into the dark water. Back and forth the grappling hook was pulled across the well's bottom. I watched silently and intently as Daddy laboriously tried to snag an object, (but hoped he wouldn't). This operation was not explained to me, but I knew exactly what was taking place. Thinking back on this traumatic incident, I wonder why I was called on to witness it.

After a considerable length of time, Daddy seemed satisfied that Floyd's body was not in the cistern. I shudder to think of how I would have reacted if things had happened as I was beginning to envision them. The planks were carefully put back over the well's opening and Daddy and I returned to the house. I think my father felt he had done about all he could do to find his son. We would all have to wait on the providence of God. *"Oh, how helpless we mortals are."*

Before concluding, "The Search for Floyd," let's go back and look at some important events that occurred just prior to my brother's disappearance. It all began like this: Floyd and my brother Cecil arose and as boys very often do, they discussed what they might do. They decided to go fishing. Their spirits were already aroused and the morning's dew had not yet evaporated. Two boys, their hooks and poles and a can of worms—what more could you ask for?

However, there was one small matter that had not been considered. It was our father. *He* had other plans for the would-be anglers. A large field of corn had recently been planted and was now about two inches high. A close observation revealed numerous "skips", that is, areas where the grain did not germinate or corn-loving crows had dug up the seed. Supplied with bags of corn and two hoes, the crestfallen brothers were instructed to replant the "skips". They well knew this would be a lengthy undertaking. There would be no fishing this day.

The two unhappy farm boys went off to the field. Thoughts of *"No fishing or cool dips in the creek,"* went through their disgruntled minds. Cecil, with his ingenious knack for circumventing his appointed tasks, suddenly stopped. Like a bolt out of the blue, he was struck with a brilliant plan—or so it seemed to him. Fishing and swimming prospects were looking up. He quickly unfolded his course of action to his excited brother. *"We'll plant a few grains on each row along the edge of the field. When Daddy comes out to inspect, he'll think we did the whole thing!* Floyd was quick to give his approval of his brother's masterpiece plan. The boys hurriedly finished their self-appointed task and returned to the house to inform Daddy.

Our father was not an academic whiz. His education was basic, as was that of his peers. However, a dummy he was not. You would have to be extremely bright to put one over on him. Going out to inspect the cornfield, the boys' chicanery was quickly discovered. As my brothers strolled along behind their father, they sensed they were going to be found out. As accusing glances were exchanged and mumblings abounded, both knew the "jig was up". *What a dumb idea anyway, how dumb can you get,* they grumbled between themselves.

Returning to the house, a whipping of some magnitude was administered. "If he beats me I'll run away from home," Floyd avowed. The two brothers received what was, in my father's eyes, appropriate for their devious doings. And so it was that my brother, Floyd, ran away from home.

Floyd had gone to Offie Jones and was given food and shelter. When Daddy arrived, he was told that they had not seen his son. Interestingly, Mr. Jones probably never knew the extent of our Daddy's hatred; in fact, he may have thought Daddy liked him. Three days after Floyd ran away, he returned home. I can safely say, we all rejoiced greatly – and that included Daddy!

"This my son...was lost... and is found.
And they began to be merry."
- LUKE 15:24
- SUGGESTED READING: LUKE 15:11-32

~ Our Dogs ~

During my childhood, few if any farms in our area were without dogs. These animals served many useful purposes. For example, as watchdogs, no stranger could approach the house or barns without being detected. "Old Rover" would sound the alarm and well might do more than that. Keeping fox, weasels and raccoons from ravaging our chicken house or killing snakes, rats, mice and an occasional "possum" was all part of Fido's service. From Daddy's point of view, a dog's worth would be determined by its ability to hunt for rabbit and squirrel. Even the mangiest old cur could be taught to hunt, to some extent. Owning a dog was never an expensive proposition as they were largely fed table scraps. The dog would sometimes augment his meager fare by catching small animals and eating them. There never were any fat canines around our house lest they lose their willingness to hunt. About the only thing we purchased for our dogs were worm pills and maybe some flea powder. We would de-tick the animals ourselves, a chore that often fell to me.

If memory serves me right, we had a total of six dogs during my youth. I remember the names of five and the order in which we owned them. A brief sketch of several is forthcoming but first let me emphasize the following point. They were not pets per se! Dogs were never allowed inside our home, nor were they permitted on the porch. No special shelter was provided for them, unless they were ill. But woe be to the soul who abused one of our animals! Daddy would not spare the offender's person.

~ "Old Jack" ~

Jack, like all the dogs we ever owned, was a mongrel. He would never sport a blue ribbon or win any kind of award, but he was gentle and he was a friend. My guess is that Jack lacked hunting skills and this fact did not sit well with Daddy. Old Jack was probably living on borrowed time.

Large, white with black spots and showing traces of shepherd, shetland and spaniel ancestry, Old Jack was quite the dog. I remember riding him when I was maybe four. It's possible he was around when I was born. A little kid would become attached to such a delightful animal, don't you think?

On a beautiful summer day, Daddy and Mama announced that we would visit our half brothers outside of Hazlehurst, a distance of about 18 miles. At the time, we had no automobile, so the journey would be by wagon, pulled by our mule, of course. These trips were fun. Going to a town and visiting our kinfolk was about the most exciting thing we ever did. My guess is that it would take us about two hours. Riding along on tree lined dirt roads, we occasionally came to washouts. Heavy rains often made passage nearly impossible. Cars, which we rarely encountered, would have to turn back. A wagon and mule were a definite advantage. Then there was that old rickety, wooden bridge, covering a huge snake infested creek and swamp. It was built with pilings and planks. As mule and wagon lumbered across, the boards would squeak, shake, rattle and rumble. What's more, there were no side rails on that miserable structure. I just knew we would fall into that inky water below us and drown.

Jack, who accompanied us would run along the side of the wagon, dart off into the thick woods and reappear minutes later. He seemed to thoroughly enjoy himself even if he didn't know where we were going. What was important to him was that his friends were nearby.

Arriving at our half brother's home, we spent several joyous days. My nephews, who were about my age, were fun. When the time came to depart for home, we received shocking news. Old Jack would not be coming with us. Carl had taken a liking to the dog and asked Daddy if he could have him. Carl was decidedly Daddy's favorite and would deny him nothing. It was done then, Jack would stay. Needless to say, the ride home was a sad one. Old Jack, our friend, had been taken from us.

Once back home, we resumed our daily routines, but something was missing and we knew it was Old Jack. No happy, frisky friend was there to brighten our day. No wet, sloppy tongue to lick our sweaty hands. Time wore on but we had not forgotten. *Then one day it happened!* Down the road he came, trotting, then loping, then running as fast as his sore feet and weak body would let him. *It was Old Jack and he was back!* We were all so happy to see our friend again, and I know the feeling was mutual.

Later on, the trip was made again and Jack went with us as before. Once more, Carl asked for the dog. And again Daddy granted his request. The pain of parting with one so dear to us returned. We could only hope that Jack would come back to us as he had before—but this was not to be. One day we received a letter from Carl stating that a car had run over poor Jack and killed him instantly. The tragic news was devastating. He was just an old dog with no special talents, but he was our dear friend and we would never see him again.

After reflecting a bit on what I have written about Old Jack, I realize he did have a remarkable talent—this lowly dog brought joy into the lives of little children.

— "Mutt & Jeff" —

Like the cartoon characters they were named after, Mutt and Jeff could usually be found together. Whether hunting, playing, eating or sleeping, they were pretty much insepara- ble. The dogs were brought to our farm while still puppies but approaching adulthood. Jeff was a tan colored mongrel hound with typical long floppy ears. Mutt definitely had the look of a coonhound with his black and tan hair. Mutt grew to be an excellent hunter and all-around good dog.

If you read the story about "The Old Rattler" you know Mutt and Jeff were involved. The snake had been driven into a copse of small trees and bushes and was under attack by our family, the sharecropper, and our two dogs. Mutt and Jeff darted in and out of the bushes where the deadly reptile had sought refuge. Eventually Daddy shot the deadly snake. This ended the extremely exciting but scary event. After we returned to the house, we noticed that Jeff was present, but where was Mutt? As the day wore on, we became increasingly concerned about Mutt's absence. I'm sure we were all think- ing the same thing.

Quite some time had elapsed when we saw Mutt coming up a little road by the side of our house. He was walking awk- wardly, stumbling and staggering as he tried to make his way home. We rushed to assist Mutt, knowing full well our worst fears had become a reality. The rattler had bitten our dog. Mutt was taken to the front yard where he was to be cared for. Daddy obviously had treated snakebites before. He began issu- ing instructions to various family members. Mama was to fire up the stove and melt a couple cups of lard. Two boys were to go to the pasture and find some cocklebur leaves and be quick about it. One of us was sent to the barn for croker sacks. Mama was further told to heat some water. The tone of Daddy's voice left no doubt in our minds as far as haste was concerned.

Upon examining Mutt closely, we could see the snake's fangs had struck him on the bony muzzle or "snout" as it is sometimes called. We might note here that a rattlesnake controls the amount of venom it injects into its victims. While hunting mice, a small amount is used. *This snake was furious. His life was being threatened!* You better believe he intended to deliver a lethal strike, discharging most of its poison. It was good that Mutt had been bitten on his hard snout. If the strike had occurred elsewhere on his body, he well might have died earlier in the day.

The croker sacks were placed under and around the sick and listless animal. It almost seemed that our efforts would prove useless because Mutt was looking bad. When the boys returned from the pasture with the cocklebur leaves, Mama placed them in the pot to boil. When the lard had melted it was given to Daddy who, with help, forced the dog's jaws apart and began pouring it down Mutt's throat. I thought, if the poison didn't kill our dog, *the lard surely would*. When the cocklebur leaves had boiled for a few minutes and cooled somewhat, Daddy began pouring the green looking liquid down poor Mutt's throat once more. I sincerely hoped Daddy knew what he was doing.

We moved Mutt out to one of our barns and placed him just inside the door, facing outward. The floor was about two feet off the ground and when the door was opened, you could see Mutt staring out at us. Water and food were placed in front of him but he made no effort to partake. *This was one sick dog.* The following morning we hurried to the barn to check on our patient. What we saw was shocking—*unbelievable!* Mutt's face was almost double its normal size. He was so pathetic looking. The next day the swelling had increased. We were certain Mutt's face would explode if he didn't die soon. Things were not going well for Mutt.

Several days went by with no significant change. Then, to our surprise, we noticed little improvements. The swelling was going down and Mutt began to eat. Gradually the good dog regained his strength and amazing as it was, he eventually showed no effects of his ordeal.

The final episode involving our dogs, Mutt and Jeff, is both sad and tragic. The family had spent a most enjoyable day in the fair city of Baxley. Being country folk, just viewing the sights and observing its citizens, believe it or not, was scintillating! It was still very light when we started for home. Approaching the house, we could see Old Jeff out by the road. The dogs always excitedly rushed out to meet us anytime we returned home. But as we drew closer, we could see that Jeff wasn't moving. He was dead! We made a quick search for Mutt his companion of many years. He was found out behind the smokehouse, lifeless as well. There was plenty of grief to go around as we mourned the loss of our two loyal friends, Mutt and Jeff.

So how and why had our dogs been killed? An arsenic laden biscuit tossed to each animal would quickly bring about his or her demise. As to why they were killed I can only speculate. My guess is they were chasing a distant neighbor's chickens or cows. Giving poison to troublesome dogs was not uncommon. Dogs ran loose on farms and, like ornery boys, often got into serious mischief when away from home.

Other Memories

~ The Missing Watch ~

We had observed the routine many times but never grew tired of witnessing it. The act's every movement seemed calculated to leave Floyd and me mesmerized. It wasn't so much the actor that intrigued us *but what he produced*. His watch simply fascinated my brother Floyd, and to some extent me. We would see him pause momentarily and remove the shiny gold timepiece from a little pocket at the top of his trousers. A small gold chain ran from the watch to a belt loop where it was securely fastened. Holding the watch in the palm of his hand, the stem was depressed and a lid that covered the watch face popped open. After noting the time the lid was clicked shut and with a very distinctive air, the beautiful gold watch was returned to its former resting place.

Back in the days of my childhood, owning a gold watch was a status symbol. If you were anybody, you owned one. (Property owners were required to pay tax on gold timepieces.) Floyd and I had never touched a gold watch, much less owned one. We were definitely nobodies.

As you have no doubt guessed, the intriguing watch belonged to our father. It was one of his prized possessions. This status symbol was immensely important to him and not to be handled by careless offspring.

Tobacco curing time arrived at our farm and our family quickly became involved in the process. Mama, my two older brothers, and a host of hired hands were busily engaged in bringing the tobacco from the field to the tobacco barn. Daddy, overseeing the operation, would assign specific duties to each worker. Each of these became a vital link in the chain. Everyone was actively involved. All, that is, but my brother and me. More than likely we were serving as water boys, in which case, there would be lots of idle time and opportunity to be inside the house.

As we were passing through the parlor, my brother spied Daddy's watch on the fireplace mantle. Arrested in his tracks, Floyd knew this was what he had long awaited. The urge to check out that timepiece was overpowering, he simply could not resist. Floyd carefully removed the watch from its resting place and began examining it up close. Popping the lid was next in order, which he promptly did by pressing the winding stem. The cover flew open, making that little "flump" sound so familiar to our ears. We could now see the crystal, so clean and clear and beneath the glass was the "oh so white" dial with ornate numerals thereon. With each tick, a thin little second hand gracefully moved around the dial. You could see the pleasure and satisfaction radiating from my brother's face. You could feel it as well. He was savoring this moment and it was an exciting one. Daddy need never know of what was taking place here. *It would be our secret, my brother's and mine.*

I am convinced that every act of disobedience has a consequence. The Bible tells us "we shall reap what we sow". *Daddy's gold watch was off limits and Floyd and I were very aware of it.* We both deliberately disobeyed him. Even though it was not my idea to handle the watch, I was nevertheless *consenting* to it being done.

The gold timepiece would never return to the mantle from which it was taken. What Floyd and I so greatly admired slipped through his fingers and fell to the hearth below, shattering the crystal! What had only a second before been an ecstatic moment for us suddenly became a time of gloom and despair. What to do? What to do? The enormity of this devastating situation overwhelmed me. I do not suggest that Floyd had a devious mind, but he was not quick to panic. He knew all too well the severity of Daddy's whippings and would devise a plan to escape them. He was not long in coming up with a course of action. We were in trouble, *big time* and a big time solution was called for. If there was no "corpus delicti," where was it and who took it? With so many people running around, anyone could have made off with the watch. The next step was to hide it. What seemed to us like an ideal place was soon found. A loose board, just under the sill of our bedroom window, was pulled back and the watch was dropped down between the outer and inner walls. Pushing the board back in place, we hoped this would be a solution to our problem.

After disposing of the "body" Floyd wanted to dig it up again. We returned to the window and pulled the board back. Reaching down between the walls, Floyd could not locate the watch. An attempt was made to peer down into the darkness but we were unable to do so. A light was needed. We found a long stick and lit one end of it. The results were *disastrous*. The window curtain caught fire and soon the wall was ablaze. Smoke began to rise up from the side of our house. Someone at the tobacco barn spotted the smoke and in no time a host of would-be firemen were dousing the flames with water. The fire was extinguished and thankfully there was only minor damage.

I believe it was after this close calamity that Daddy discovered his watch was missing. He became furious, accusing the hired hands of stealing it. I have no doubt he threatened to kill the crook that had stolen his gold watch. You can rest assured that two frightened boys were not about to "fess up". What is most amazing to me is that neither Floyd nor I were punished. We both fully expected to be whipped to within an inch of our lives.

At some point in time, Floyd obviously became deeply convicted about the recent events. Clearing a troubled conscience is good for the soul. Courageously, he asked Daddy if he revealed where his watch was, would he not be whipped. He was assured he would not. The hiding place was pointed out. Once more our father was reunited with his precious gold watch, shattered crystal and all. That status symbol seemed to mean everything to him.

Today Daddy's watch is displayed in the home of my nephew's widow, Boots Land of Hazlehurst, Georgia, the place of my birth.

— Turpentine ("Turp" In Time) —

Sitting in front of me as I write is a small bottle containing gum spirits of turpentine. The oleo—resin derived from the beautiful Georgia long leaf pine tree, was produced by the last turpentine "Still" in the United States. In 1925, the year of my birth, Baxley, Georgia could boast of having the largest Still operation in the world. After the Civil War, the South's moneymaker was "King" cotton, but we hasten to add that turpentine sales would also help keep food on many a poor man's table.

Ten thousand trees were considered a crop. Small farm owners would be doing well to have five hundred trees on their property. Daddy and other farmers leased their trees for a year to the large Still operators. They received about one dollar per tree. This extra income was greatly needed, especially in the thirties.

Turpentine has a very distinctive odor. There is not another smell quite like it. The sap from which the "turp" is made has many names. Some call it tar (pine tar), rosin, resin, gum or pitch. In times past, boat builders used the sticky resin of the pine tree to waterproof their vessels. In Genesis 6:14, God told Noah to build an ark of gopher wood and to "pitch it without and within". The pitch or pine tar, as a southerner likes to call it, would keep Noah's craft dry inside and afloat.

Turpentine had, and has, many uses. At one time it was the primary thinner for many paints. In medicine a rectified type is used in making liniments and astringents. Around our home "turp" was used for a number of things. My brothers and I "went barefoot" most of the time, and frequently stepped on nails. Mama was quick to douse the punctures with turpentine. Cuts were treated in a similar way. Should a family member develop the "slows", a combination of sugar and turpentine would definitely speed things up. Plasters were sometimes made using "turps". I can't truly say it helped but at least we all survived.

In 1875, Texas fever was rampant in Baxley, Georgia. J. Isham Carter, a reporter for the "Eastman Times" who covered Appling County, came down with the dreaded malady. Poor Isham decided to "doctor" himself. He began by chewing pine tar and drinking a pint of turpentine. I'm happy to report that Isham did survive! My brothers and I often chewed pine rosin and sap from the sweet gum tree. None of us seem to have suffered any ill effects from this practice. You may disagree after reading my poem inspired by Isham.

If with a fever you suddenly come down,
Don't head for the doctor in a nearby town.
Just hasten to the woods where you'll find it free,
A chunk of rosin on a big pine tree.

Now chew it and chew it like it's bubble gum,
I think you'll discover it's helped you some.
Friend, if you will take a little "turp" in time,
That nasty old fever will cease to climb.
So then from your bed you will certainly jump,
To stand on your head on a big pine stump.

- BY RAY LAND

~ The Intellectual ~

He stood in the shade of the beautiful pink flowering crepe myrtle that adorned the yard. The shrub, profusely ablaze with its colorful blossoms, seemed an appropriate backdrop for what was forthcoming. My brothers and I sat at his feet intently listening to every word that poured from his lips. This, our brother, having gone abroad, had returned to us. We were enthralled when he spoke of his adventure, and utterly amazed at the maturity he was exhibiting. Our brother had gone away a boy and returned a man.

I can still see my handsome brother Kenneth as he posed under the crepe myrtle, one hand firmly grasping a limb, just above his left shoulder, the other resting on his right hip, with palm facing outward. It would not have been thought too manly, to position one's palm on his hip. Southern boys were taught to never appear effeminate. Back to "the intellectual."

Kenneth attended the old Altamaha school. Only six grades were taught in this scholastic institution. He graduated in 1929. Mama, who had taught at Altamaha, thought her son should receive further schooling. In 1930 or 1931, arrangements were made for him to attend school in Lyons Georgia, more than 30 miles away. Once there, he would obtain room and board at the home of an acquaintance of Mama's.

When it came time for Kenneth to depart for Lyons, our half brother, Carl, arrived from Hazlehurst to transport him in his big truck. Much to my delight, the entire family would be making the trip. As soon as all was ready, we piled onto Carl's old truck and off we went. After about six miles of dusty dirt roads, we reached U.S. Highway Number 1. Pulling onto the paved surface, we headed north.

I should like to point out that there was little or no development along this stretch of the road. In fact, we would seldom encounter another automobile. What you would see were trees and bushes, squashed turtles, squashed snakes and more bushes and trees. There would be no comfort station, in the event nature called. Hey! This was the ride of a lifetime and my sibs were ecstatic. If a trip to the woods became necessary, we would be right at home in them. Now as for the ladies, that would be a different story.

We had crested a hill and were starting down a long descent. Up ahead, a passenger car had stopped in the road. Our curiosity was momentarily aroused but as we passed the vehicle, everything became quite clear to us. An elderly women was squatting down behind the side of the automobile and a very long stream ran down the road. We laughed until our sides ached. To young boys, this was a sight to behold. At last, we arrived in Lyons where Kenneth would enroll in the seventh grade. I really don't remember whether we were happy or sad, maybe a tiny bit of both.

The late fall and winter months seemed to quickly pass by and spring was rapidly approaching. Soon school would be out and our older brother would be home. We could only wonder if he might have changed. Would he be the wiser for having improved on his three R's? It was certain he would have every opportunity to excel at his three P's when he returned. "What on earth are the three P's," you ask. Why, just a cotton farmer's basics: plowing, planting and picking.

So there he was, standing right before our very eyes and looking ever so impressive. I didn't know what a Philadelphia lawyer looked or sounded like but I'm sure my brother fit the bill. Sporting a blue chambray shirt, denims and an old felt fedora, Kenneth cut quite a figure. Even though his trouser legs were a mite short, those tanned bare feet looked terrific. Ordinarily my brother's attire was "Sunday go to meeting clothes" but, since he was "grown up" they were for every day.

As we sat looking up at Kenneth, one of my brothers asked him a question. A simple yes would have sufficed but his reply was not to be so elementary. He responded with a positive and authoritative *"Absolutely!"* Oh, wow! What a big word. My brothers and I were awed by just the sound of it. I think we understood our brother's response was an affirmative one, but absolutely? *Absolutely!*

~ *Face to Face* ~

It was fun to make tunnels in the hay and stored cotton. Crawling along the tight passages was an adventure with a degree of fear. A combination of fun, adventure and risk made for an exciting time. One day I learned what it was like when the fun part ceased and only the fear factor remained.

On a regular basis Mama would roll up the huge linoleum rug in our parlor. She would tie strings around the ends of the rug and place it out in our yard. Mama would then proceed to scour the parlor's wooden floor with lye. On one such occasion I was playing in the yard. In time, I spotted the "ready made" tunnel. A quick glimpse told me I quite possibly could squeeze through the rolled up rug. As with the hay and cotton, all the elements for an exciting time were present. Traversing that long, dark tunnel would be an adventure not to be passed up.

Kneeling down, I poked my head inside and began edging my way forward. I discovered rather quickly that reaching the other end would be no easy task. The stiff linoleum had no give and progress was slow—and there was little wiggle room. At this point in my travel, I don't remember what I was thinking. Backing out did not appear to be an option.

People frequently speak of a mid-life crisis or a decisive turning point. I now was about mid way in my journey, when I made a startling discovery. *I was not alone in this pit of doom!* It seemed my heart would pound a hole in my chest. As I peered into the dim light ahead of me, I could see it moving. Suddenly I was face to face with a snake! Fear, panic and claustrophobia set in big time. The harder I struggled, the more difficult my situation became. If that snake caught up with me, I was a goner! Finally the end was reached and I took off screaming for my Mama.

~ The Toothbrush Tree ~

Sometimes Mama would say, "Raymond, go get me a toothbrush." Now where do you think I would go to obtain this item? For sure it wasn't the bathroom. A trip to the swampy woods was necessary. Once in the woods, I knew exactly where to find "toothbrushes" for they grew on trees. The black gum, also known as sour gum, pepperidge and tupelo trees, grew in abundance on our farm. Locating a young tupelo, I cut long twigs off the horizontal branches. The twigs were about six to seven inches long and about the thickness of a pencil.

When I returned from the woods with a handful of "toothbrushes", Mama would peel about one inch of bark off the stick's end. Then she chewed the end of the twig until it turned into bristles. Dipping the toothbrush into a mixture of one part salt and three parts baking soda, sparkling white teeth were the result. Sometimes ashes from the fireplace were also used to clean teeth.

By the way, do you know that tooth decay is the most common disease to man? I have taken the liberty of calling the black gum a "toothbrush" tree but there really is one called the "toothache" tree. The prickly ash is so named because its bark produces a cooling sensation when chewed, and acts as an anesthetic for toothache.

It should be noted that my Grandma used her "toothbrush" for something other than cleaning teeth. She would pour snuff into the palm of her hand, wet the brush and proceed to rub the snuff over her gums and teeth. I frequently saw snuff dippers doing this and enjoying it.

~ *Coleman's Demise* ~

The solemn faced messenger arrived bearing shocking and tragic news. Our half brother, Coleman, had been struck by an automobile and was seriously injured. Daddy began immediately making plans to leave for Hazlehurst. His eldest son laid suffering and a father's place was at his son's bedside. My mother accompanied Daddy, leaving my brothers and me at home.

The details concerning Coleman's accident were sketchy and it would be some time before a clear picture emerged. As you may have surmised from reading this story's title, it is destined to have a sad ending. In many ways "Coleman's Demise" was the conclusion to what had been some of my happiest days, and some of the more sorrowful ones as well. Now as Paul Harvey would say, "Here is the rest of the story."

Mama and Daddy arrived home to their eagerly awaiting offsprings. They must have been surprised that no mischief had taken place. The graveness of Coleman's condition had obviously subdued our spirits. We were apprised of events leading up to the terrible accident and those that followed.

On Sunday evening (March 25, 1934) Calvin, our beloved nephew, and his father were returning home from Hazlehurst. About a mile from town, their automobile began to experience motor problems. Coleman pulled their vehicle off to the side of the highway and stopped. As it had not yet grown dark, Coleman began examining the automobile. Soon a car was seen approaching at a rapid speed. As it drew near it began to swerve directly at Coleman. My half brother's reaction was to jump on the running board of his car to escape being hit. Sad to say, this did not save him. The oncoming car was so close that a protruding door handle struck Coleman in his side. Flesh was torn from his body as he was violently thrown to the highway. His leg was broken in several places. Calvin, not yet 10 years old, could only watch, horror stricken and helpless as mortal wounds were inflicted on his father.

An unknown Samaritan took Coleman to the private hospital of Dr. John M. Hall—an outstanding surgeon. The good doctor used all his skills on Coleman's side and leg. He would tell a family member he thought the leg might be saved, presumably from amputation. By mid-week and after Mama and Daddy had returned home, Dr. Hall discovered that Coleman had extremely serious internal injuries. On Friday, March 30, 1934, John Coleman Land died. He was 38 years old.

The perpetrator of the dastardly act that took the life of Calvin's father would go unpunished. His father was a prominent citizen of Hazlehurst. The driver maintained it was an accident. He said he was out driving with friends and did not see Coleman until it was too late. No charges were brought against him. Coleman's body was brought in a coffin to the home of his brother Carl. Our family came to view the body and stayed overnight.

That night as Calvin and I lay on a pallet, our thoughts were focused on the open coffin in the parlor below. We were frightened and sleep would escape us. We huddled together, whispering to one another. At any moment we expected some kind of ghost would enter our room. What then? What would we do? At last our tired bodies and troubled minds succumbed to the blessing of sleep.

The next day the body was taken away and soon thereafter Calvin and his family departed for Alabama. I would not miss Coleman so much but I cried and longed for my nephew. Perhaps I thought we would never meet again. We do not know what a day may bring forth, be it good or evil, but God is in charge and as the Good Shepherd will continue to love and care for His sheep.

After 1934 it was 50 years before I saw Calvin again. When we finally met at a family reunion, I was sadly disappointed. No longer was my beloved nephew the little boy I loved to play with and also share our pain and sorrows. He had the same name but he neither looked nor acted as I had remembered him. A man stood before me and shook my hand, but it wasn't "Calvin". I can hear a frightened young boy crying out in the night with a pleading voice saying, "Please Daddy, don't kill him, don't kill him."

Calvin Lee Land departed this life August 30, 1988.

"A friend loves at all times, and a brother is born for adversity".
- PROVERBS 17:17

— Gone Forever, The Wild Plum Thicket —

When the sad and mournful day came when I would leave the old farm place where I had spent the first ten years of my life, an uncertain future lay ahead of me. I could only wonder with much anxiety, how it would play itself out. My family, a way of life, and the world as I had come to know them were being dissolved. To those wiser than I and definitely more perceptive, the tragic, memorable day was as inevitable as death and judgment. Never again would I romp and play with my brothers in the stored cotton or hay. No more fabulous rides to the watermelon patch in that old sled, stuffing our pockets with scrumptious pecans or eating our fill in the wild plum thicket. Jumping out of the hayloft doorway with a homemade parachute would cease to happen. Many happy times had been spent with my siblings but those childhood pleasures would no longer be shared together. While I did not know it on that fateful day, our family, in its entirety, would never be together again. *So much that had been a part of me was destined to be forever lost. Only the memories remain.*

After 18 years of a tumultuous, combative and seemingly loveless marriage, my mother and father separated. Poor, dear Mama could no longer endure Daddy's physical and verbal abuse.

It hadn't entered my mind that Mama would one day leave Daddy. Penniless and trapped in what appeared to be a hopeless situation, only divine intervention could solve Mama's dilemma. At last Providence smiled down on my dear mother. Leonidas Love Clay, a Presbyterian minister and Mama's great uncle died. He left his estate to Mama. "Uncle Bud" as he was affectionately known, had acquired little of this world's goods. A true pilgrim, "Uncle Bud" would endow his favorite grand niece with two lots in California, two old trunks and a few hundred dollars. By today's standards, Mama's inheritance was "small change" but to Mama it was a fortune.

Mother was quick to seize upon what she perceived to be an avenue of escape. The first step was to purchase an old car. My brother, Kenneth, would be able to drive it. Unbeknown to most, if not all the family, Mama responded to an ad in a farm publication. A landlord was seeking a sharecropper family. Acting covertly, all the arrangements were made. I'm sure Mama thought she had found the opportunity she had long sought. If her plans came to fruition, she would be free! Free from an insanely jealous husband. No more would Mama have to listen to false accusations of infidelity. Hopefully she would at last find a measure of peace. Strange as it may seem, Floyd and I do not recall the actual departure. Were there no farewells? Was Daddy not angry? Could he be privy to Mama's plan but was helpless to stop it.

Seeking a better life for herself and her children and having an old car, a few dollars, and some personal belongings, Mama and her brood of five embarked on what would be for them a long and thought-provoking journey. As we made our way along, Mama must have shared some of the details of her plan. At least a clearer picture of our future began to emerge. Thanks to youthful optimism and enthusiasm, the bleakness of our situation was not all that apparent. But we were destined to become what was commonly called, "poor white sharecroppers". Our destination was a small farm outside of Jackson, Georgia, about 160 miles away. None of us had ever seen the place or the man who owned it. No matter—our faith was in Mama, and there our hope and love would repose as well. From the youngest, Faye age 3 to the oldest, Kenneth age 17, our mother was the primary object of our affection; she was our stay. The course had been determined, we had set sail and there was no turning back.

— From the Frying Pan Into the Fire —

We arrived in Jackson quite late in the afternoon. It had the typical look of a small southern town. Being the county seat, a rather stately courthouse was situated on the square. The trip had been long and tiresome leaving us weary and famished. Mama's priority, however, was not resting or feeding her offspring, but getting to the farm before dark. She made a few food purchases in the A&P and inquired as to the farm's whereabouts. Once more we got underway. In a matter of a few minutes, Kenneth brought the car to a stop in front of a very unimpressive looking dwelling. "Could this be it?" we well may have wondered. As we gazed on what now would be our home, I think reality set in. We were all stricken with a severe case of nostalgia. Mr. Kimball, the landlord who was expecting us, soon made his appearance. He was distinguished looking, wore laced boots and displayed a kind of ruggedness. You got the impression he was a no-nonsense individual. How my crafty brothers would fare in dealing with this transplanted Canadian remained to be seen.

Thankfully, the house was furnished which was a definite plus because we had brought only our clothes with us. The landlord lit a kerosene lamp and proceeded to show us the interior. We could all agree that this place would never win any "Good Housekeeping" awards. Mr. Kimball who lived in a little cottage about 75 yards away, bid us goodnight and returned to his home.

This had been a very long and trying day for all of us. Mama, the dutiful and caring mother that she was, hastily prepared a meal for her flock, made our beds and sent us off to dreamland. Tomorrow would be another day.

~ Misgivings ~

A desperate but resolute mother and her five children soon discovered their new world was not a paradise. If, per chance, they had entertained thoughts of finding a utopia, this notion was quickly dispelled. The farm was disappointingly small, about one-fourth the size of the old home place. Two shabby, weather-beaten barns housed the animals, hay, grain and what farm equipment there was. The house was unpainted and the interior dark and dreary, giving its inhabitants a foreboding feeling. I would be remiss not to mention a most important edifice, the outhouse, a two-holer, complete with path. One old mule, two or three cows, a few chickens and a dog made up the livestock.

One feature that impressed us initially was a pecan orchard, several acres in size. Would you believe it? Not a single pecan was produced in all the time we lived there. Nuts? Or should I say, no nuts!

With all the despairing remarks about our surroundings I must point out a very important factor relating to our situation—we were all safe, together and our beloved mother stood like a strong tower in our midst.

Mr. Kimball, the hearty and robust looking landlord, exhibited a very powerful personage. There would be rules for the vassals, and we would be expected to obey them. It might be that we would hearken unto the commands of his lordship, if Mama so ordered. Mr. K. rarely deviated from his daily routine. Arising early in the morning, he would go outside to the well. A stand was there with a wash pan and a pail of water resting on it. During winter, ice would form on the water's surface. Breaking through the ice with his fist, the pail's contents were poured into the wash pan. Mr. K. would then begin sloshing the water, crystals as well, over his face, neck and hair, rubbing vigorously! All the while the "Brrrr!" sound was loudly heard. Sometimes Mr. K. would take a razor from his pocket and shave.

Following his wash-up, he briskly pranced down to our place and seated himself at our table. There, he would be served a steaming bowl of cracked (rough ground) wheat. The wheat grains had to be soaked overnight before cooking. Evidently Mama had agreed to the landlord having his breakfast with the family. This intrusion into our private life was tolerated but definitely not wanted.

As time wore on, Mr. K. would take liberties, commit acts and make requests, evil in nature, upon family members. Mr. K's coup de main was a threat to shoot my brother, Cecil. What our mother had hoped would be a new and promising beginning would end in disaster and despair.

"Boast not thyself of tomorrow..."
- PROVERBS 27:1

~ The New School ~

Floyd and I fully expected to attend school in Jackson, some two miles away. Although the hamlet was small, having a population of about two thousand residents, it would be exciting just to be in town so often—definitely a treat and something we were unaccustomed to. But much to our disappointment, our school destination would be a little whistle-stop with a population of around two hundred. For all I know, that number may have included the dogs. The school was four miles distant. My brother and I would walk two miles and catch a bus for the remaining two.

~ Butch The Bully ~

There is usually something memorable about your first day at a new school. Maybe a cute little girl with freckles and curls would look at you and smile. Could be you were embarrassed by comments about the patches on your overalls. You may

even have fallen in love with your beautiful teacher.

On my first day at the new school, we all filed out onto the playground at recess. Scarcely a minute had transpired when the school bully stuck his face in mine and began making threats. It was clear my peers were siding with this fellow, for they began to shout, "Hit him, Butch! Hit him!" I had not supposed that this was the way newcomers were officially greeted, but I had learned the name of my adversary. Those gathered around continued to urge Butch to slug me, which he obligingly did. Pushing me to the ground, he sat astride my stomach and continued to hit me in my face, much to the delight of his fans. I guess Butch grew tired of dealing out punishment, for he eventually gave it up. The alpha bully had once more demonstrated who the playground chief was. All the pounding was quite unnecessary, I had not sought any position, nor would I ever.

As I lay on the ground, having my facial features rearranged, I did not feel animosity towards my assailant—for some reason I had not fought back. I was puzzled by the behavior of both Butch and the other children. *Why were they angry with me? I had done them no harm.* They were all strangers to me. It was all very perplexing at the time. It's been seventy-two years since that schoolyard incident, and I'm still perplexed.

> *"...when He (Christ) was reviled, He reviled not again;*
> *when He suffered, He threatened not..."*
> - I PETER 2:23

~ *The Greedy One* ~

Having suffered a most humiliating and demeaning experience at the hands of an obnoxious Bully, my self-esteem was nonexistent. I was convinced no one liked me. This had become painfully obvious on the playground. It may have been that I was hoping for a way to enhance my image, if so, opportunity came knocking.

A number of older boys were circulating among the new and younger students, inviting them to participate in a kind of grab bag game. Those desiring to play were to put anything of worth found in their pockets in a sack. Pennies, tops, knives, plug tobacco tags (a choice item) would be welcomed. During the noon hour, the promoters of this game of chance would take those participating to a ravine in back of the school. A dense thicket and trees would obscure everyone from the teacher's eyes. This kind of activity was strictly taboo! Once at the spot, a clearing was made to dump the loot and cover it. Players would be brought to the scene and told to position themselves around the pile. On a count of three, the covering would be quickly snatched away and eager participants were to grab whatever they could.

It was all so wonderfully exciting. I was not allowed to play marbles for keeps but nothing had ever been said about grab bag. Producing some object from my pocket, it was deposited in the sack. Now we would anxiously and excitedly await the dinner bell.

At last what the young gamblers were listening for sounded. We quickly rushed to the appointed place. I may have thought this was the opportunity to impress my peers. I was quick, with my keen eyes and speed, I would make off with the bigger portion of the goodies. We were instructed to kneel down and wait for the countdown. Finally it began! One two three! The covering was rapidly snatched away. Eight to ten grasping, greedy hands were thrust like rockets into the pile. As quickly as they went in, they were pulled back! Yucky yuck! Our hands were covered with the smelly mess. *We had been tricked.* Our eyes no doubt expressed our anger but there was nothing we could do. The older boys ran away laughing. Soon the other students, at least a good number of them, would be told. They would look at us, hold their nose and snicker.

This time my shame and degrading experience was self-inflicted. Those who had perpetrated this ruse were not responsible for my involvement. Greed had been my motivator.

~ The Model T ~

On our way to school, brother Floyd and I would pass a little farmhouse. Neither the inhabitants nor the house itself were of any interest to us. What did get our attention was an

old Model T Ford that sat in the yard. Day after day we would see the flivver quietly sitting there. Weeds grew up around the solid rubber tires. It was obvious the decrepit, topless old car was ready for the junkyard. Did this aged relic beckon us to rescue it from the heap? Somehow we could not pass by without looking at that "tin lizzie". Floyd, being a compassionate soul, began to feel pity for the pathetic wreck.

The day finally came, (and I knew it would), when we stopped to make inquiry. "Is that Model T for sale?" My brother asked the black gentleman. "Yes" was his reply. "You can have it for five dollars." We thanked the man and moved on. Floyd didn't have five cents, let alone five dollars. The story of the old Model T could have ended upon hearing the price but it didn't. Floyd wanted that automobile and was determined to purchase it. "Where, pray tell, will he get the money?" I wondered. I have always admired my brother's cunning ability to make a buck. I hasten to add, an honest dollar.

Back in our childhood there were two ways a young boy might earn five dollars. It would be an extremely difficult task but it could be done. You could sell the Grit newspaper or Cloverine Salve. I distinctly remember my industrious brother selling that cure-all balm about that time. The money in hand, Floyd went to the farmer's house to make the purchase. We knew the car wouldn't run but we were surprised to learn it had no motor. My brother took this bit of information in stride. He was, after all, the owner of an automobile. That fact alone would greatly enhance his status.

Floyd now faced an almost impossible challenge. The car was his but how would we get it home? There was but one answer to this important question. We would have to push it. Our house was roughly three quarters of a mile away. Not such a long distance but about one half mile would be up a hill. We pushed, we sweated, we groaned and then we rested. We pushed, we sweated, we groaned and then we rested. This action was repeated over and over. At last we arrived at the bottom of the hill. Our hardest work still lay before us. By now I was wondering how my brother could be so dumb. Five whole dollars for a piece of junk! But "where there's a will there's a way". Floyd had the will for sure, and we eventually made it home.

This seems like a good time to end this story but, as yet, there had been no fun. So I have to continue. Floyd began immediately to strip down the car. Out came the seats, radiator, and windshield. Off came the doors and fenders. Finally nothing was left but the frame, wheels, steering column and gas tank, which was located under the front seat. The whole process must have taken several days. The stripped down model was now ready for action. I soon learned what Floyd had in mind for his car. We began pushing it out onto the road. This task was relatively easy. Several hundred pounds had been removed from the Model T.

We reached the top of the long sloping hill. Floyd took his position behind the steering wheel, sitting on the gas tank. We were now set for the ride of our lives. My brother gave me the signal to start. I gave our vehicle a big shove and jumped up on the gas tank beside him. Down the hill we went, faster and faster! It was the thrill of a lifetime. You could feel the wind in your hair, on your face and in your teeth! We were grinning from ear to ear! *I ask you, what could be more fun?* This was one super ride. At last we reached the bottom of the hill and slowly came to a stop. We sat there for a time looking at one another and congratulating ourselves. The experience had been exhilarating. This ride would long be remembered! Now our story has come to an end, well, almost anyway. There was the matter of getting back up that hill. We pushed, we sweated, we groaned and then we rested!

~ Miss Clara ~

Clara was the daughter of a tolerably well to-do farmer, whose wife just happened to be the landlord's sister. Most importantly, Miss Clara was my teacher. You might think that because of these relationships I would have it made. Surely she would cut me some slack—you know, let up on the reins. For reasons I didn't understand, this dream did not materialize. Instead Miss Clara treated me with disdain. Nothing I did seemed to please her. My mother, having taught school, made certain our homework was done but when my papers were turned in, they were given a quick glance and promptly marked with an F. It was Miss Clara's contention that Mama had done the work. Needless to say, I was rapidly losing interest in anything related to the educational process. It was my sincere belief that Miss Clara despised me. The following episode is offered as evidence for my suppositions.

Our class had assembled on the playground. The teacher formed us into a circle, and we began playing "Drop The Handkerchief". The air was filled with 'oohs' and 'aahs' and shouts of joy. Each of us, no doubt, was hoping the handkerchief would be dropped behind us, so we could give chase. As a runner breezed by, I took a quick peek, saw the 'kerchief, grabbed it and took off in hot pursuit. The idea was to tag the other runner before he reached the spot I had vacated. It all seemed so simple but one of us had mistakenly changed directions, as we would soon discover. About mid way around the circle we collided head on! Nose to nose. We both fell to the ground, momentarily dazed. Blood began spouting from our noses like a water fountain. The other fellow, after seeing the blood, began screaming at the top of his voice. Instantly, I knew I was in serious trouble. This blubbering lad was none other than the teacher's pet, and a relative no less. Miss Clara had witnessed the terrible accident and was on the scene immediately. She began shouting, "Look at what you've done! Look at what you've done!" or words to that effect. I was ordered to remove myself from her presence by going to the restroom to clean myself up, while she lovingly and tenderly began focusing her attention on her little darling. Once back in the classroom, Miss Clara told me I would have to stay after school as punishment for my reprehensible deed. And what's more, the erasers were to be dusted and the blackboard washed. It wasn't enough that I had missed my bus and would have to walk home. Then there was the business of explaining my conduct to Mama. Would she understand? That was the big question.

~ Hooky, Happy and Hopeful ~

As the days rolled by, I became less and less interested in schoolwork. I was always glad when my brother and I missed the school bus. Instead of walking two more miles to school and being late, we would decide to play hooky. That was always exciting and a fun thing to do. It wouldn't be if Mama found out, but we were willing to run the risk. Floyd would write notes to the teachers and sign Mama's name. Usually we were caught doing this bit of chicanery and punished. Our attitude was largely, so what? Hey! I said it was fun.

I was nine and in the fourth grade when I was enrolled in the new school. Within three months, I had grown to despise the school and anything associated with it. The only friend I had was brother Floyd and I may have wondered if he would be there for me, should I call on him.

When playing hooky in the wintertime we would look for a secret place to hide. A dry, sunny field was the most desirable, if there was tall grass and weeds. A spot would be flattened out and a fire started. If Floyd had any smokes or chewing tobacco, that would be super. We would eat our dinner when our stomachs signaled. An occasional hooky would do wonders for our sagging spirits. Strange as it all may seem, those hooky-playing times were some of my happiest days, together with my brother, there in a field, with no one to mar our peace. We would look up at a bright blue sky and watch the changing shapes of fluffy white clouds as they slowly passed by. Lying on the ground with our eyes turned heaven ward, we would dream of far off places and of good things we hoped would someday come.

Instead, one day the sad news came from Daddy, telling us that the old home place had been sold and another farm had been purchased or leased. It had also been decided that the three younger children would take turns staying with our father. Faye, not yet four years old, was first to go. I would be next.

During the 1934-1935-school break, I departed for Hazlehurst. My emotions were mixed. I surely didn't want to leave my dear Mama, but I would have no say in the matter. On the positive side, I would be attending the same school as my beloved nephews, Julian and Curtis. This prospect would be a comforting factor. Most of my brother's hopes and dreams as well as those of my own would never come to pass. Neither of us mourns the fact that great things did not come our way. Instead of our dreams being realized, it was those of our beloved mother that enriched us. She desired that my brother might know the Savior and that I would trust Him as well. By the mercies and grace of a loving and compassionate God, we now await the coming of our Lord and Savior Jesus Christ, who is our hope.

"Seekest thou great things for thyself? Seek them not."
- JEREMIAH 45:5

~ Eureka ~

To the best of my knowledge, I had never been separated from my mother. No, not even for a single day. Now, tragically, the time had come when I was being sent away. For me, home was where Mama was. Leaving my dear mother for the first time and at the green young age of ten would be a very emotional experience. I was certain to cry often and long for her presence. There was another unsettling aspect to the separation: Mama was consenting to it! The thought that Mama would willingly send me away was devastating. Insecurity and distrust would result and trouble me for a good portion of my life.

My brother, Kenneth, would drive me to Daddy's farm. As we drove along all was not gloom and doom. One happy prospect awaited me at our destination. My three and one half year old sister, Faye, would be at Daddy's.

I don't recall my reaction upon seeing the farm, but one thing is certain, no one would be impressed with its appearance. The house was a typical "sharecropper's" shanty. One small barn, a chicken coop, cow shed and privy made up the outbuildings. Other than one milk cow and a few chickens, no desirable creatures were visible, not even an old mule.

Kenneth would return to Jackson with Faye on the day of his arrival, so Daddy gathered my little sister's things together and placed them in Mama's car. Waving goodbye, we watched as they sped off down the highway and disappeared from view. As I stood by the front steps of that little shanty, it seemed like I was being deprived of *all that was dear to me.* I longed for my little sister; I ached to see my precious Mama! At last, I looked down at the ground. There in the sand was a spool and snuff can. This was where Faye had been playing and the two items were her toys. At that moment, I experienced a kind of grief that I would never know again until I witnessed my mother pass away. Somehow my father must have sensed the agony of my soul. He said nothing. It may be that my old Daddy was feeling the same pain I was.

Following the departure of Faye and Kenneth, a brief period of mourning ensued. No one had passed away but one may well have thought so. It was evident from the look on my father's face that he truly loved his little daughter. I had never witnessed such an expression before and what I saw was good. This moment was to be savored while it lasted. Reality would set in soon enough and it surely did.

The evening was approaching and there were chores to be done. The cow would have to be fed and milked. Since it was winter, wood must be chopped and brought inside for the fireplace and stove. These tasks and others would become my responsibility. Daddy made our supper. Most of the time it was cold cornbread and milk. At times leftovers would be the fare. When green vegetables were in season, Daddy would cook a big pot of beans and okra. Invariably, this slimy concoction would burn, much of it sticking to the bottom of the pot. It tasted awful, but I was compelled to eat it.

In the mornings the chicken feed was scattered about in front of the coop. "Old Bossie" was milked and fed before I took off for school.

With memories of "Butch the Bully" and my antagonist, Miss Clara, racing through my mind, I approached this new seat of learning with some trepidation. It was extremely comforting to know that Carl's two sons, my nephews Curtis and Julian, would be fellow students. This just had to be better I told myself. After all, the school had such a wonderful sounding name. Eureka!

Archimedes, the great Mathematician, is said to have shouted "Eureka!" upon making an important discovery. The word means, "I found it!" The State Motto for California is "Eureka" for obvious reasons if you think of the "gold rush."

Arriving at the school, the milling students all seemed friendly enough. Miss Pennington, our teacher, was ever so pleasant. Had I found what many look for? A utopia? But looking back on that new beginning, a simple eureka would suffice.

Miss Pennington seemed impressed with my class work as well as my attitude. The dear lady even spoke of advancing me to the fifth grade. I dare say I had become the teacher's pet. This was certainly a new experience for me and I loved it! There was little doubt but what my head size had increased dramatically.

One day, Julian told me about a huge rattlesnake that had been killed. It was lying along the roadside and I would see it as I walked home. Be it dead or alive, a rattlesnake causes me to have a fit of nervousness. In other words, they give me the "willies". Standing and peering at the reptile, I could feel the hair on the back of my head and neck crawling. Something told me to move on but I did so want a trophy. I found a sharp stick and pried the rattles from the lifeless carcass. Then I folded them up and put them in a matchbox. The next day I took my prize to school and showed them to my classmates. They were all duly impressed with my show n' tell object. The bell rang and as we filed in a brilliant idea struck me. *What a great gift my trophy would be for my teacher.* She would think me generous and so brave. Without hesitation I quickly went to her desk and placed the box on it. After all the children had come in, the teacher seated herself to begin calling the roll. Then, she spotted the matchbox. Curious, Miss Pennington opened it. Out flew the rattles as our teacher jumped sky high, letting out an ear-piercing scream! After managing to compose herself somewhat, she angrily shouted, "Who did it? Who did it?" Immediately all heads turned in my direction. A loud chorus of "he did" rang out. That was it then—a pet no longer, no more talk of advancement. Hey! I would be doing well if I even passed. It was all so well meaning and innocent.

Miss Pennington went on to teach school for many years. She was honored and loved by a host of her students. I attended Eureka School for a total of four months and pretty much enjoyed my time there. Oh yes, I passed the fourth grade with flying colors. On one of my trips to Hazlehurst, I had hoped to visit with Miss Pennington, but sadly the esteemed lady had departed this life and I was told she had gone home to be with her Savior.

"In Thy presence is fullness of joy; at Thy right hand there are pleasures forevermore."
- PSALM 16:11

~ The Gypsies ~

The day was drawing to a close as Daddy and I sat quietly on the front porch. Mostly we just looked and listened. Outwardly, we were a picture of peace and serenity. Inwardly, well, that was another matter. My thoughts most likely would be about Mama, Faye and Floyd or tomorrow's mischief. I can only wonder what my father was thinking.

Although a major highway ran by Daddy's small, mean dwelling, relatively few cars passed by. At days end we could hear the sound of an automobile miles away. As we sat there leisurely we began to hear vehicles approaching. The hard rubber tires created as much noise as the engines. Shortly after hearing the noisemakers, not one, not two, but a virtual caravan loomed into view. Both Daddy and I leaned forward attentively. An assortment of cars, trucks and trailers began to slow as they neared our place. The lead car pulled off to the side of the road and stopped, as did the other vehicles. A man got out of the first car and began walking toward us. Although I had no idea of what the dark stranger wanted, I was pretty sure he was a Gypsy. Even though I had never seen the likes of this nomad before, nor any of his kind, tall tales of thieving Gypsies were frequently heard. Visions of being chopped up or stolen away filled my thoughts. Politely greeting us, the stateless wanderer asked Daddy if he and his clan might camp in our field for the night. After considerable wrangling, Daddy agreed to let the Gypsies stay overnight. The fee was fifty cents.

The gate to a large field that adjoined our yard was opened. One by one, the motorcade drove in and parked. Immediately, and I do mean immediately, doors flew open, fires were started, flambeaus and lanterns were lit. Tables, benches, pots, pans and who knows what else appeared. Surprisingly, chickens in crates accompanied these migrant folk. An old hen would be decapitated, de-feathered, disemboweled, potted, plated and devoured in record time. There was constant shouting, singing and talking, both before and during their meal, not to mention the yapping canines. A joyous spirit seemed to prevail amidst the madness.

After supper the gaiety and frolicking began in earnest. The musicians played rollicking tunes as the singers and dancers performed magnificently. Everyone was having a splendid time, including yours truly. I think Daddy was enjoying himself too, but I might have been wrong. The festive activities would end about as quickly as they had begun. All at once the lights were put out and silence fell over the camp. Only a few remaining coals from the fires continued to glow.

Back in the house, my distrusting Daddy had loaded his old shotgun, pocketed his Colt 32 pistol and parked himself at a window. From this position, he could observe any movement within or without the Gypsies bivouac. He was determined that there would be no pilfering this night. I stayed up for a time but finally went to bed.

The Gypsies were up at the crack of dawn, eating and loading their vehicles. They were surprisingly quiet during the whole process. Within minutes, cars and trucks were started and these very unique people had driven out onto the highway, to continue their wanderings. There was little to indicate anyone had spent the night in the field. All the trash had been picked up and dirt raked over the fire ashes. Daddy seemed pleased with the past night's events. *That is, until he counted his chickens!*

— *Curtis* —

Curtis Land was the son of my half brother, Carl. During my stay with my father in 1935, we had bonded and spent many happy days enjoying each other's company. Our likes and dislikes were similar. We shared our joys and sorrows together. There were two years' difference in our ages but this was never a factor in our relationship. Two additional things of importance impacted our lives. The first was we had austere fathers and the second was we had sinful natures. We would learn early in life that engaging in acts of disobedience results in dire consequences. We both engaged in an act that did not meet with our parents' approval. Let me tell you about it—

Carl operated a garage and gas station. He also sold soda pop, candy and tobacco products. An open box of cigars was prominently displayed on a front counter. Passing in and out of the station, almost on a daily basis, Curtis and I took note of the cigars. If I'm not mistaken, they sold for five cents each. Many times I had puffed on cigarettes, chewed tobacco and even dipped a little snuff. Curtis on the other hand, had done little more than take a puff. Older boys would tell us, "You ain't a man till you learn to smoke". That meant inhaling. Puffing didn't count. Seeing those big, beautiful cigars and sniffing their aroma would prove too invitin' to Curtis and me. One day, when everything looked favorable, we removed a "King Edward" from its nesting place. The next step was to get it down to Daddy's without being caught. This was done and we began waiting for an opportunity to fire that baby up.

Curtis and I had stolen but our conscience was not troubling us. In fact, we may well have been congratulating ourselves! The ideal moment to enjoy that pilfered stogie finally arrived. The two of us were alone at Daddy's. I retrieved the cigar from its hiding place and taking some matches, went out into the pasture. We found a nice grassy spot on the side of a little slope, well out of sight of any prying eyes. Neither of us knew that the round end of a cigar needed to be cut or bitten off in order for it to ignite. We lit match, after match, after match and took turns drawing on the cigar but nothing happened. Somehow, quite by accident, we must have chewed the end off and smoke began to flow through. At first we would improperly draw on the King Edward, getting smoke down in our lungs, causing us to gag and cough. We were, however, determined to smoke that cigar, and we did—all of it. Lying on the grassy knolls' slope, we became two sick boys. Sick to the point of barfing! Consequence had caught up with us and oh, how we did pay!

"Let him that stole steal no more."
- EPHESIANS 4:28

~ The "Would Be" Hobo ~

Back in the days of steam locomotives, especially during the 1930's, we heard the saddest, and most mournful (or shall I say melancholy) sound to fall on mortal ears. It was from the whistle of a great steam engine. As trains rumbled along the rails at night, their sorrowful cry would reverberate throughout the countryside. To those who heard its wail, strong emotions were evoked, not the least of which would be loneliness and nostalgia. This legendary sound was immortalized in song and was often referred to as "the lonesome hobos squall".

When Curtis came to stay overnight, we would lie on the floor and listen to the train whistles. It would make us both sad. Curtis missed his beloved grandmother. The dear woman had been a factor in his coming to know the Lord Jesus as his Savior. For me, it was my Mama. I was very homesick for my mother and my siblings. I repeatedly told my nephew that I would one day "hop a freight", but I never did.

After returning to the Jackson area it would be over thirty years before we saw one another again. Curtis said he had always told folks I had "hopped a freight" bound for Jackson. More than likely, when he didn't see me around, he assumed I had.

> *"Oh that men would praise the Lord for His goodness, and for His wonderful works to the children of men!"*
> - PSALMS 107:8

~ Bon Voyage (Farewell) ~

No one could have convinced me that going to live with my estranged father would be anything short of a nightmare. The thought of spending time alone with him, in the same house, was frightening. For the better part of a year, I would be under his scrutiny, day and night. It would be impossible for me to behave that long, I reasoned. Daddy would not have four sons to keep an eye on, just me! Nothing would escape him.

But amazing as it was, I don't recall receiving any whippings during my stay with Daddy. Throwing rocks at hobos, stealing and smoking a cigar was about the extent of my criminal activity. Floyd might think I had reformed or developed some of his skills. After all, I had been his number one disciple.

Addie, Curtis and Julian's stepmother, was wonderful. She showed me much kindness. The sadness and loneliness I experienced were softened by this dear lady's thoughtfulness. It was fun and usually exciting to be around Curtis and Julian. The latter seemed much more mature than myself, even though he was only a year older. Could be his mischief was much more sophisticated than that of my own. The boys' little sister, Carlyne, always reminded me of my own little sister, Faye. It was easy to transfer my affections to Carlyne to help me cope with my pining for Faye. Probably the person to have the least impact on my life was Carl. This half brother just simply ignored me. Better this than to be bouncing my head off the highway like Coleman had done some time previously.

Life with Daddy had not been all that bad. Fact is I was rather enjoying my stay when the day came for me to make another move. This time it would be to Mama and my little school.

~ Out In The Cold ~

Upon returning to school, my nemesis was waiting. Miss Clara would be my fifth grade teacher! Woe is me! I don't remember much of what went on that year, but one incident stands out—yes, it was negative, as usual. A schoolmate and I were caught playing "tic-tac-toe" during class. Our punishment was to remain in the room at lunchtime and play 500 games of 'tic-tac-toe'.

At the end of the school year I was told I had failed. Flunked! I must confess there was justification for the failing grade. It was bad enough that I didn't pass but to be told Miss Clara would be my teacher for the coming term was hard to take. When fall rolled around the outcome remained to be seen. I had no realization of it at the time but serious trouble lay ahead for Mama and her offspring. The dark clouds of doom and despair were forming on the horizon and headed our way.

One day when Floyd and I were in school, the horrible storm struck! Mr. Kimball ordered Mama to take her belongings and leave his farm at once! Threats to have authorities enforce his demand were advanced. What was a poor woman to do? She had no mule, no wagon and worse yet, no place to go. My brother Kenneth had used most of our mother's inheritance money for a failed gas station deal. To make matters worse, he ran off and joined the army and took her car with him.

We managed to get an old mule from somewhere—probably a kind and sympathetic neighbor. Soon what little goods mother possessed was loaded into the wagon and Mama, Faye and Cecil climbed on and started to drive it away. At this juncture Mr. Kimball appeared and demanded that an item in dispute be unloaded. Both Mama and Cecil insisted the contested piece was theirs and once more started to leave. At this point the irate landlord brandished a pistol and threatened to kill Cecil if he moved the wagon. Needless to say whatever was being argued about was surrendered, without comment, I might add.

In some unbelievable way, Mama found an old farmhouse to rent. It was in Locust Grove, a small community some ten or more miles away. All of the above events took place while Floyd and I were in school. I believe Cecil came for us, when school let out. We were shocked and flabbergasted by the news but delighted as well. We would not miss our former landlord. Besides, there were never any nuts on those lousy old pecan trees, anyway!

Trust in the living God, who is the Savior of all men."
- I TIMOTHY 4:10

~ Out of the Cold ~

The first query posed to man by his Creator was "where art thou?" It is well we did not ask ourselves that question. A quick assessment of the family's situation could best be described by one word, "desperate". It was winter and the old house was cold, drafty and dark inside. No wood had been cut for the cook stove or fireplace and one might say "food was scarcer then hens teeth". With minimal bedding, keeping warm that first night was difficult, to say the least. With four hungry mouths to feed and little or no cash, dear Mama would be hard pressed to provide for us. What an awful load she was obliged to carry! As a child I didn't have great concern. Mama was with us and that's what mattered to me.

Within a day or two of our heartless eviction, Mama walked into Locust Grove, and caught a "local" train into Jackson. Thankfully, she was able to find work at a green pepper cannery. The pay was "chicken feed". Hey, beggars can't be choosers, so no one was squawking. Mama took our little sister, Faye to work with her everyday. Floyd and I were attending school.

Kenneth, having failed as a filling station proprietor and seeing mama's $300 go down a rat hole, had left for Fort Benning some time previously. He now was attired in olive drab or khaki. Cecil was the next to leave, maybe with Mama's best wishes. If I am not mistaken, he took off for Hazlehurst to our half brother, Carl's, place. He later also became one of Uncle Sam's recruits. As I have said, our situation was a desperate one. Who could blame the boys?

During our brief stay in the Locust Grove area, we witnessed one of the south's worst ice storms. Practically everything was frozen over. Phone lines, electric lines and trees were down. Huge limbs broke off and roads and streets were blocked. Traffic snarled. People in Atlanta had no electric or fuel. Those with fireplaces began burning their chairs, piano stools, tables and any other wood they could lay their hands on to keep warm. Floyd and I tried to walk into Locust Grove. I should say we slid or skated. A waist high privet hedge ran along the side of a big mansion at the little "burg". Somehow Floyd got up on top of the frozen solid hedge and walked its length. The ice supported his weight. It was amazing.

A few weeks after the Kimball fiasco, who should turn up but our Daddy! My brother and I just knew a reconciliation was in the works and colloquially speaking, "we 'uns shore were agin it". Daddy proceeded to talk Mama into moving to Alabama, where he owned an 80-acre tract of land. He purposed to build a new house there. Mind you, my father was now 75 years old. I suppose anything was better than what she had and with Daddy making all kinds of promises, Mama consented to go with him.

Some days after Daddy's visit, an old truck, loaded to its gills with Daddy's belongings, pulled up to the house. Mama's goods were then piled on top of what was already a mountain. It looked to me as if the vehicle and its load would topple over. At last everything was set. Floyd and I had somehow found a spot and squeezed ourselves into it. Mama, Daddy, Faye and the driver took their places in the cab. The old truck was started and with a multitude of creaks 'n squeaks off we went, looking very much like a scene from John Steinbeck's film "The Grapes of Wrath." We were bound fo' Alabama!

> *"What therefore God hath joined together,*
> *let not man separate."*
> - MARK 10:9

~ *Moving on Again* ~

Once more we had sailed off on a rather long voyage—a journey we all may have hoped would bring us to a land of contentment. Were our faint hopes destined to disappointment? What awaited us on that distant shore? Only God knew what lay ahead. But none of us were thinking about leaving our destiny to God. That is, none but my little sister Faye.

Our dear, impoverished mother, in a well-meaning attempt to secure a more wholesome existence for her children, had failed miserably. Daddy, promising reform, had come back into her life and the lives of some of her offspring. Mama was compelled to capitulate. If there had been another way out of the burdensome dilemma, she would have taken it.

Stuffed, uncomfortably, down among a ton of household goods and farm equipment, Floyd and I could barely see the scenery as it flashed by. Even though we had no radio to entertain us, the old truck would oblige. A harmony of sounds fell on our ears. There was a constant whine of the vehicle's tires and the rhythmic beat they made crossing expansion joints in the road. From the motor came an assortment of whirring and purring tones. Crescendos and diminuendos were reached at every hill. Then there were the melodic notes of the wind as it whistled around us. The combination of all these marvelous sounds produced a virtual symphony. The wonderful music was haunting and nostalgic, and at the same time, it was exciting and promising. Brother Floyd and I would experience a wide range of emotions as we huddled down in our tight quarters.

As we traveled, a number of "pit stops" were made for gas, oil and water, etc. One very unexpected stop resulted when our driver drove under a rather low bridge. Thankfully we were not going too fast. The load did not clear and suddenly there was a loud crashing crunching sound! The truck was stopped immediately! Other than being scared out of our wits, Floyd and I were not injured. An old rocking chair was the only casualty. After a long and tiring day, we finally arrived at our destination. The house Daddy had leased was quite nice. The next day we explored the farm.

> "...He shall gather the lambs with His arm,
> and carry them in His bosom..."
> - ISAIAH 40:11

~ The Last Stand ~

We had come to the Romulus community and moved into the old Griffin house. Mama and Daddy were no strangers to this area, having lived there in 1917. Why Daddy chose to return to this particular locality was, at the moment, of no interest to me. As long as Mama, Faye and Floyd were close by, I would enjoy a small measure of peace and contentment.

A new school was being constructed and the old one was soon to be torn down. Some classes were held in the New Hope Baptist Church building. Floyd and I began attending the Romulus School shortly after our arrival in the community. Much to our delight, no hostility was shown to the "Georgia crackers". One of my classmates and I became friends immediately. We had similar sounding names. His was Raymond Landcaster. He reminded me a lot of my bosom pal from Altamaha School in Georgia. I believe there was a quick bond between us because we were both introverts, and not surprisingly, dull! I only knew Raymond for one year but during that time, ne'er a cross word passed between us. He was my friend and I was his. We moved away from the Romulus community and I never saw or spoke to Raymond again. Over sixty years rolled by without hearing one word about my long lost school buddy.

One day I was visiting a pal of mine in Holt, Alabama and somehow during our conversation Raymond Landcaster's name surfaced. My friend said he once worked with Raymond. For a brief moment, a surge of excitement and joy swept over me. It has always amazed me how many thoughts race through our minds on occasions like this. Leo then told me the sad and shocking news. Raymond, my friend, had been killed in an automobile accident in 1951. I can't quite explain it but I felt the loss of my friend ever so keenly. I'm reminded again of the Scripture: "A friend loveth at all times" Proverbs. 17:17.

More and more of Daddy's plans were manifested as time wore on. He would buy 80 acres of land from old Jim Knox who was a highly respected mulatto and son of a former slave. The property was located in a very remote section of the Romulus district. It was here Daddy would build his house. Many additional purchases were made such as a mule, milk cow, pigs and chickens.

A wagon was an absolute necessity for Daddy's agricultural pursuits but they were expensive. Some serious thought would be given before Daddy would shell out money for anything. At last and for only a few dollars, my enterprising papa turned up with what loosely might be described as a wagon. The components were there but the "thing" was laughable. The vehicle had a bed, sides and seat fastened to an old automobile frame. Attached to the frame were two axles with four wheels sporting solid rubber tires. It wasn't pretty but it definitely was very functional. With the mule hitched to the "thing" it served many useful purposes. I loved to go places and drive our old mule and wagon. It may have been embarrassing to Daddy to be seen in it. He was, after all, a proud man.

The rented farm and our newly acquired acreage were about two miles apart. We would cultivate both properties, if our backs held out. Several acres of new ground were cleared of trees, bushes and stumps. Daddy, Floyd and I worked long and hard getting the ground ready for spring planting. Lucious Thomas, a dear Christian Brother, was of immense help in all of the farm work.

Daddy sold a large portion of the timber to the paper mill and a lumberyard. A crew of men came with their sawmill, cut down the magnificent trees and sawed them up into planks. We retained enough of the sawed timber to cover the outside of Daddy's proposed house. Lumber, doors and windows from the old Romulus school would be bought to complete the project. By the end of the school term, our family would be fully ensconced in our new abode, be it ever so humble. We planted corn and field peas at the Griffin place and cotton on the newly cleared ground. Mama had started a large garden and would sell her vegetables at the curb market in Tuscaloosa. We had enough watermelons and cantaloupes to start the saliva flowing, plus a big patch of peanuts.

By all outward appearances, things were going extremely well. Undeniably, we had much to be thankful for. While we waited for harvest, cash was in short supply. With Daddy, "tending the store," Mama and I found work on John Graham's farm. We began chopping cotton, one of my most objectionable tasks. Mama was to receive $.75 per day. My wage was $.50. After Mr. Graham saw the results of my day's accomplishment, he lowered my pay to $.25. Most of my time in that hot old cotton patch was spent with one bare foot resting on a knee while leaning on the hoe handle. Floyd had found employment, cutting cordwood. You can bet he did not fare much better than Mama and I did.

Two streams ran along the sides of our property. One of

them was fairly deep. Daddy got the bright idea of seining the deep one for fish. The creek could best be described as a snake pit! No one but the foolhardy would traipse up and down that reptile alley. The banks were lined with bushes, shrubs, trees, overhanging vines and limbs. Little to no sunrays penetrated the thick foliage. Even though the creek water was very clear, it looked jet-black.

The seine or net was rolled up on two long poles. By unrolling and rolling up you could adjust your net to the width of the creek. Floyd and I made our way down to the least congested area and jumped in, bare feet and all. The water varied in depth, running from waist to arm pits. Floyd and I unrolled the seine and slowly edged our way along. We poked the net up against the bank all the while keeping a sharp eye out for those dreaded reptiles. Daddy, armed with shotgun, leather boots and carrying a bucket, presumably to put fish in, weaved his way up the creek. Every so often he would ask us to raise the net. It usually contained snakes, eels, sticks, crawfish, frogs and minnows. When we complained about the snakes and our fear of being bitten, Daddy would say Cottonmouths couldn't bite you under water. Need I tell you how frightened we were? It was a most horrifying experience. Even Daddy, with boots and gun, must have been scared. Well, it was all for naught. There would be no fish fry this day. My brother Floyd does not remember this seining episode. He must have been more frightened than I thought.

One of our neighbors was a black man named John L. At least, I think that was his moniker. He was a powerful, big man, soft spoken, hard working and honest. He might be described as a gentle soul. Our subject was in a sense, self sufficient, since he owned his own farm. It was about three "hollers" from our own. If you desired to go there, you would cross one of our fields, go the length of the cow pasture, through a stretch of woods and then across said neighbor's fields to his house.

One day John L. arrived home to find his wife in the embrace of another man. He was horrified at the sight of his spouse's infidelity! He became so ENRAGED that she would defile herself—losing all sensibility and having a revolver on his person, John L. drew it and shot the unfaithful wife. She died instantly. The authorities came soon and arrested the distraught husband. A trial was held and John L. was sentenced to only one year in prison. There were mitigating circumstances you see and southern justice was kind to a man who had been made a cuckold.

John L. served his time and returned to his home and resumed farming. He planted a large cotton crop but when it matured, he realized picking it all himself would be nigh on to impossible. Help was needed. John L. decided to throw caution to the wind and seek that assistance.

The big, black man stood in the yard with hat in hand and respectfully asked to speak with Daddy. He explained his situation to my father and pled for help. Daddy would not physically be able to pick a lot of cotton, so would be unable to come to the neighbor's aid. Mama, hearing the conversation, offered her services and much to my chagrin, those of mine as well. Strange as it seemed, Daddy gave his consent for Mama to help John L. with his cotton picking.

For several days, Mama and I made our way over to the neighbor's cotton fields. When it came to picking those white fibers, Mama was superwoman. She could out pick most men, including John L. Every day about eleven thirty Mama and I would return home. Daddy's dinner was prepared and then it was back to the cotton field. I asked Faye, who sometimes accompanied us, what she did when at the work site. "Oh," she said rather lackadaisically, "I probably sat in the shade and played." I may well have thought she ought to have been picking cotton herself. Then again, I may have thought something else.

One afternoon as we were returning home from the neighbor's farm, I spied a little bird perched out on a leafless limb. Picking up a small stone, I tossed it at the feathery music maker. And would you know it, the rock struck God's little creature and it fell to the ground, lifeless. This was no ordinary bird; it was a bluebird. When Mama saw what I had done, she became emotionally upset. Like many Southerners I have known, killing a bluebird was a bad omen. Misfortune would surely befall you. She was absolutely right about that. In less than two minutes I was given a tongue-lashing and a good thrashing! Talk about retribution—it came quickly.

In all probability it was Saturday and we had all had gone into town. Upon our return, Daddy took a leisurely stroll out by the big barn, something he customarily did after having been away for a few hours. Once he passed the barn, he spotted Daisy, our milk cow. She was lying on her side and barely breathing. Her stomach had swollen to an enormous size, so much so that her feet were off the ground. Daddy came back to the house and informed us of poor Daisy's plight. Then he went to where the suffering animal lay and did what he knew to do for her. We all followed him to the tragic scene. It was depressing and heart wrenching. In spite of the steps that were taken, within minutes the bovine expired. We all mourned the passing of this noble lady. She had nourished all of us.

Daddy explained to us that Daisy had probably seen and smelled the tender, luscious, young field peas growing among the corn stalks. The animal was determined to get to those succulent green leaves and pods. She had forced herself through the strands of barbed wire and started her eating frenzy! Who would tell the dumb beast when enough is enough? One look

at her bloated abdomen indicated Daisy had been gorging herself for quite some time. Finding the cow back in the pasture
was puzzling. She may have become extremely thirsty from
eating all those legumes and was desperately seeking water.
Surely there are lessons to be learned from the actions of our
milk cow. May this be an example to all of us.

~ Steamboat Haven ~

When Floyd announced he was going to build a steamboat,
I was impressed. This would be one of his most spectacular
undertakings. It did occur to me that no large body of water
was anywhere near. Noah had built a great ark on dry land,
and Floyd would build his little steamer. "First, we will dam
up the creek" Floyd said. I'm not sure I liked the "*we*" part.
This could mean work which is rarely fun. We cut down a
few small trees and placed them across the rivulet. Mud, dirt,
weeds and bushes were piled on our dam. It all paid off for
soon we had a little pond. Two beavers could not be more
pleased with a similar accomplishment. The boat, I learned,
would not be large enough to ferry me across the pond. Despite
failing to meet my anticipation, our spirits were not damp-
ened. The steamboat's bottom was made of tin, the sides of
wood. Two rows of bricks supported the boiler, which was an
old gas tank. Only a few construction steps remained. A hose
was run from the boiler to a hole in the stern. The hose would
protrude below the water level. This would be the steamer's
propulsion system.

At last the boat was completed. We should have christened
her "The Floyd" but we didn't, just one of many oversights.
We were not "nautically minded". We dragged Floyd's pride
and joy down to the pond for her maiden voyage. A fire was

built under the boiler and we sat anxiously waiting for steam to appear. Considerable stoking had to be done but eventually it began to pour out the propulsion tube. It was now launch time. We pushed the craft out into the water and held it. No sense in letting it get away from us! The old boiler was producing steam galore! The skipper turned our vessel in the opposite shore's direction. In a second we would see the fruit of all our labors.

Cast off! Floyd and I released our hold. The bubbling water with steam rising up was loud! *But the USS Floyd barely moved.* Had we blown on the steamer's bow, I think it would have gone backward. A pessimist might have viewed our endeavors as a failure, a complete waste of time. Brother Floyd and I totally reject any such conclusion. We learned a number of positive things from the boat-building project—first of all we learned how to construct a temporary dam and pond, and second, we learned how NOT to build a steamboat. Most importantly we learned that "if at first you don't succeed, try and try again."

~ The "Little Puff" ~

As a child I liked to smoke. It was a pleasurable thing to do. My siblings introduced me to the practice in an indirect way. It was monkey see, monkey do. Smoking was a means of escaping our immaturity and entering into adulthood. It was not necessary that tobacco be used for smoking. Coffee, corn silks, dry cotton leaves, grape vines and "rabbit tobacco" would work just fine. Place your choice ingredient on a piece of brown paper, roll it up, twist one end and you would be ready to light up. I hasten to add here, that if Mama or Daddy caught us carrying or using tobacco, we would be severely

punished! There would be times when my little sister and I were left home alone. Who was watching who on those occasions was debatable. One day while Mama and Daddy were away, Faye and I were left at home alone. When our parents were gone and Faye was busily engaged with something, it seemed like the right time for me to take a smoke. Getting my "makings" together, I climbed up onto the barn roof facing away from the house. From this lofty position I would be out of the sight of searching eyes. I sat quietly and peacefully on the old barn's roof watching fluffy white clouds in a sea of blue, sail lazily by, holding my homemade cigarette between my fingers. I relaxed and allowed my imagination to transport me to exotic places.

Suddenly the serenity I was enjoying was shattered by a familiar voice saying, *"I'm gonna tell on you"*. Slowly turning my head, there I saw the face of my little sister peering over the edge of the roof. Her grating declaration was repeated several more times and the, *"I caught you"* look, with a gloating expression written all over her vindictive countenance. This was a serious matter, but I wouldn't panic. Pleading or threatening was out. Her silence had to be obtained by a sophisticated plan. Keeping cool and collected was important while I mulled the situation over. If Faye talked, Mama would "skin me alive".

"Come on up", I beckoned to my sweet little sister. "It's nice up here", I said, *my voice dripping with kindness*. It was my Sunday best shot and it worked. Soon Faye was seated beside me and I began extolling the merits of the cigarette I was smoking. "You'll like it," I said rather enthusiastically. It was evident Faye was beginning to weaken. "Just take a little puff," I cajoled, holding in front of her the crudely made cigarette. She moved her head slowly forward, puckered up those baby lips and took a little puff. *"Oh, I'm gonna tell on you"* I shouted! BUT, "if you won't tell on me, I won't tell on you", I quickly added. So a deal was struck, thankfully. My baby sister would never tell.

Faye and I chuckle when I mention the "little puff" story. She finds the incident amusing but I still experience a twinge of guilt. To deceive one you love is despicable. Then again, those switchings Mama gave were excruciating.

~ Missing Mama ~

During the summer of 1937, mother and Faye went to visit grandpa and grandma in Andalusia, Alabama. They expected to be gone about one week. The goodbyes had hardly been said when I began to miss Mama. Before the sun had set I developed a severe case of melancholia. In the early evenings, I would traipse up and down the road crying "Mama! Mama!" repeating her name over and over. It almost seemed that my heart would stop beating. As I think back on those painful nostalgic days, I definitely attribute my behavior to one thing, insecurity! But let us continue.

About a day before Mama's scheduled return, we received a card saying she was ill and would be unable to come home until she was well. This news was devastating. While Daddy was not treating me badly, he was indifferent to my anguish and heartache. I desperately needed someone who understood my pain. At last, I decided to run away from home. The people I sought out were kind and understanding people and I was confident they would help me.

The Geesling family lived about four miles from our place. When I arrived at their home, they gave me a warm welcome and patiently listened to my story, showing me much love and kindness. It was amazing how comforting these dear people could be. About the second day after coming to my friend's home, Daddy came in the wagon looking for me. One of the Geesling boys hid me in a shed while his parents spoke to Daddy. After a few minutes my father drove off. Receiving much encouragement from the Geeslings, I decided to go home and face the consequences. I had survived other thrashings and I supposed this one could be endured as well. I thanked my kind friends and started back home. Two thoughts occupied my mind as I trudged along the sandy roads. When will

Mama return and what will Daddy do to me? The answers weren't long in coming.

Drawing closer to our house, a confrontation with Daddy was raising my anxiety level. I fully expected to find him in a foul mood and ready to give me a good beating. If that were the case, he would have to catch me first. I had decided I would run away again rather than endure a whipping. But when my father saw me, he was very cordial and made no mention of my absence. I breathed a sigh of relief. There was no flogging, and not even a reprimand. And there was further good news: Mama was coming home soon! Hallelujah!

As I write about the Geeslings speaking to my father, I've wondered if they lied to him about my whereabouts. It is difficult to think these good people would utter falsehoods. But as I continue to write, a wonderful thought occurred to me: most likely my friends told Daddy I was there, and suggested he let me return home on my own volition. They well may have explained to him how distraught I had been. Who knows, the Spirit of God may have touched a responsive chord in my unhappy, old father's heart.

"A soft answer turneth away wrath."
- PROVERBS 15:1

~ *Gloria* ~

My mother was visiting a neighbor and took me along to be company for our host's little boy. Ruth Patrick was also a guest and was accompanied by her daughter, Gloria, age ten and son Richard Thomas, age four and a half. The boys and I were sitting on the ground playing some kind of a game. Gloria stood behind me observing. Out of the blue, Gloria uttered three enchanting words, *"I love you!"*

They were only three little words but she spoke them with such warmth and tenderness. Their sound was like the soft melodic call of a bluebird to its mate. I could feel the emotion in her sweet voice as my face turned crimson. My head was lowered 'til my chin rested on my chest. I dared not look back at her beautiful countenance lest the wonderful dream would go away. I never remembered hearing anyone say those three beautiful words to me before, and I shall always treasure them.

January of 1942 I left high school to join the Navy. I was 16 years old. On April 9, 1944 I was home on leave when my dear mother went home to be with her Saviour. Returning to Naval duties, I was both happy and sad—happy because the Lord had saved me and sad because the memory of mother's death was still grievous to my soul. It was during this time I thought of Gloria and decided to write her. Two letters were written with no response to either. Gloria was now 17. She may have been romantically involved and did not choose to write, I reasoned.

Some 30 or more years after the war (WW2) Ruth and I were visiting the Romulus community and made inquires about Gloria. The following is the story I was told: "One Sunday afternoon, Ruth with her daughter, Gloria, and young son, Richard, went on an outing at a nearby lake or river. Richard, who had entered the water, began to cry out for help. Gloria went to her brother's rescue but was compelled to call for assistance as well. The mother, Ruth, hearing and seeing her struggling children, attempted to save Gloria and Richard but her heroic effort failed and she too drowned.

Gloria, Richard and their mother, Ruth, departed this life May 27, 1944. The bodies of all three rest side by side in the New Hope Baptist Church cemetery in Romulus. If I could stand before Gloria's gravestone, I would say, "Thank you, Gloria," and "I love you too".

— The Final Chapter —

I do not suggest that Mama and Daddy fought daily, but over a twenty-year period of time there had been serious altercations. Daddy's suspicions of Mama continued but he did not verbalize them in her presence.

We had only been in Romulus community a short time when Daddy, finding me alone, began asking questions about my mother. "Did she speak to this or that man?" he inquired. Once he offered me what I thought would be a "pack" of Wrigley's gum for an answer, so I told him what he wanted to know. Then he gave me *one* stick. I always tried my best not to implicate Mama and probably lied. She may well have said "hello" to some man, but I was not about to tell Daddy. He became angry with me and made some drastic and unforgettable remarks that haunt me to this day. He did have reason to distrust me.

Mama made several trips to the curb market in Tuscaloosa to sell vegetables from her garden. It was there she made the acquaintance of Louis H. Wolfson, an orthodox Jew. The two became friends in a relatively short period of time. Louis was 58 years old and had never been married. He was a man of some means and fairly well known in the community. He was a quiet, intelligent and respected man. Eventually he expressed his desire to marry Mother and offered to pay for the divorce. My sister Faye would be part of the arrangement.

On December 4, 1937 Floyd left home to join the army. This was a sad and mournful day for me. I could only wonder what life would be like without my dear brother to comfort me. But, as painful as Floyd's departure was, it would pale in light of what was soon to come.

I expected another separation between Mama and Daddy was looming but was not overly concerned about it. Mama would be there and that was all that mattered! Near the end of December my parents were talking openly about their breakup. It was to be a divorce, not a separation. Then the shocker came. Faye would go with Mama, *and I was to stay with Daddy!* I couldn't believe what was happening—*Mama didn't want me—she was going to leave me behind.* I screamed and I cried as I had never done before. There would be a separation, alright, but IT would be between *Mama and me!*

My agonizing was for real and this must have touched my dear mother's heart. She went to Mr. Wolfson and informed him that he must accept me, or the marriage would be off. Thankfully my step-father to be was amenable to the ultimatum. So Mama divorced my father and married Mr. Wolfson. She lived a relatively happy life until her death on Sunday, April 9th, 1944. I saw my father only one more time for about twenty minutes. He died on August 10, 1940.

Ray and Ruth Land, married 60 years in 2006

EPILOGUE

This series of short stories about a young boy and his siblings growing up during depression times in south Georgia should not just end without a little explanation as to what became of this family.

After moving to Alabama our parents were divorced in 1937. Mama remarried and lived happily until her rather early death from cancer in 1944 at the age of 52.

The oldest son, Kenneth, served 3 years in the U. S. Army and then came to live in Alabama where he became a commercial photographer. Later on he worked as a conservation officer for the State of Alabama while still pursuing his photography interests. He married and raised two sons. He died at the age of 85.

Cecil served in the South Pacific with the U.S. Marines during World War 11. After returning home at the end of the war he married and remained in civilian life for a few years, but later rejoined the Marines, making it a career. After his retirement he had a second career with The Firestone Tire & Rubber Company. He was the father of three girls and one son. He died at the age of 83 in Georgia.

My brother Floyd also made a career of the military and retired from the Air Force at the young age of 36. This left him enough time to begin a new career as an auto parts dealer. He has one daughter and one son and currently lives in Mississippi.

After my mother died in 1944 I was sent to live with an aunt in Ohio. At the age of 12 I was put on a train, alone, for the journey from Alabama to Ohio and to a new and different world for me. I married my high school sweetheart at 19 and together we had two daughters and one son. The two girls and their husbands became Christian missionaries to Africa and Switzerland respectively. My husband was a very successful business owner. He passed away in June 2007 after nearly 57 years of marriage. Our son is following in his father's footsteps as a business owner. I still live in Ohio.

Last but not least, Ray served his tour of duty in the U. S. Navy, and upon discharge came to Ohio to be where I was living. He married a neighbor girl and to this union was born a daughter and two sons. Ray was a very talented artist and went to work for the Goodyear Tire and Rubber Company as a sign writer and cartographer. He and his wife celebrated their 61st wedding anniversary this year (2007). They presently live in Pennsylvania.

These are stories of times and incidents from Ray's incredible memory bank. He spent countless hours and days researching and retracing his steps in this rural setting of South Georgia making certain his memory served him correctly.

When all is said and done it just shows me once again how the Lord had His hand on me, and others in this family. John 10:29 says "My Father, who has given them to me is greater than all: no man can snatch them out of my Father's hand".

Faye Land Blair

Top: Faye Land Blair, age 12
Middle left: Allie Myrtle Land and Faye, 1938
Middle right: Ray's father, Stephen Land, age 79
Bottom: Ray, Curtis and Stanley Land, Altamaha School, 1964

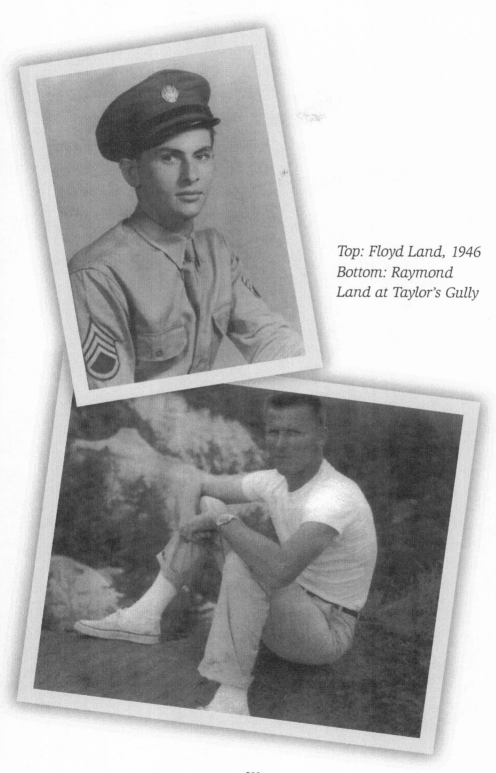

*Top: Floyd Land, 1946
Bottom: Raymond
Land at Taylor's Gully*

Ray's Mother and Stepfather, Mr. and Mrs. Wolfson, 1939

Daddy's Family

Kenneth, Cecil (3 1/2 months) and Ellie Land

Top: Floyd, Kenneth, Faye, Ray Land
Bottom: Kenneth, Cecil, Floyd, Raymond and Faye Land

Made in the USA
Charleston, SC
15 July 2010